murdoch books
Sydney | London

threebirds
RENOVATIONS

VACAY *Vibes* AT HOME

CHAPTER FIVE

CHAPTER SIX

CHAPTER SEVEN

A DECADE OF DREAM HOMES

Three Birds, THREE BOOKS! Was there ever any doubt?

This one has been a long time coming, and we couldn't be more excited to finally share it with you.

It's hard to believe that Three Birds has been flying for over ten years now! What started as a cheeky little "Hey, let's flip this one house and see how it goes" has turned into something bigger, bolder and more fabulous than we ever imagined.

Seriously, if you'd told us back at our first reno that we'd be here – three books in, countless renovations under our tool belts, and a thriving community across the globe – we'd have laughed, ordered another coffee and gone straight back to packing the skip bin.

But here we are! By the time this book lands in your hot little hands, we'll have tackled nearly 30 kitchens, over 50 bathrooms, 70-plus dreamy bedrooms and 80 outdoor areas. And guess what? While we've learned something new from every single transformation, one thing has stayed the same: the joy of creating spaces that feel like an escape.

This book is all about that magic and it's packed with vacay vibes for the home – the kind of inspiration that makes you want to turn your everyday into a getaway. Whether it's a Mediterranean-inspired villa, a modern coastal haven, a Palm Springs party pad or a moody snow-capped cabin, we've got plenty of ideas to get you started.

TRIPPY

The beautiful thing about the Three Birds brand is that at its heart, it's always been about more than just the number of women who founded it. Three Birds is symbolic of a collective of like-minded women – backing each other, cheering each other on, lifting each other up and forming real friendships through the ups and downs of renovating... and life.

That's why, this time, we've brought some mates along for the ride. Inside this book, you'll get a good ol' stickybeak into the homes of just a few of the people who make up the Three Birds community, people we know and love: our family, our friends and a few of our superstar school students.

We have over 40,000 amazing humans enrolled in our online Reno School and Styling School courses, and helping these students create their happy place is honestly the most rewarding thing we do.

The spaces we've chosen to share in this book are bursting with good vibes and ideas that'll have you reaching for your vision board before you've even turned the page.

Whether you're dreaming big or starting small, if the idea of living every day in a holiday mood speaks to your soul, you're going to LOVE this book. We've poured every ounce of passion, creativity and let's-get-it-done energy into these pages, and we cannot wait for you to dive in.

Let's make your everyday feel like a VACAY.

Love,

Bonnie, Lana and Erin
(and the Three Birds community) xxx

LIVE BEAUTIFUL
TAMSIN JOHNSON Spaces for Living
BEAUTIFUL AUSTRALIAN HOMES VOLUME IV

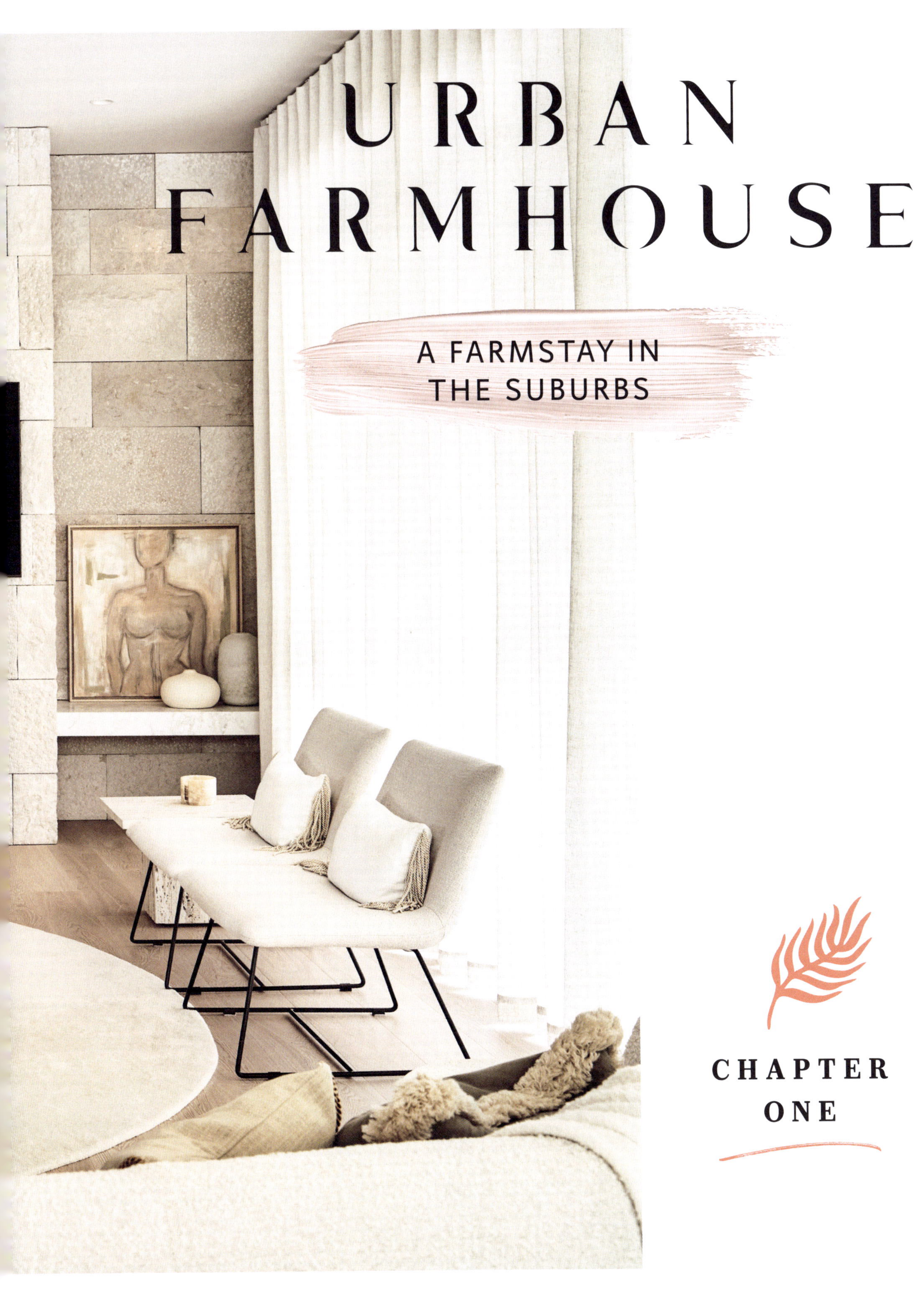

URBAN FARMHOUSE

A FARMSTAY IN THE SUBURBS

CHAPTER ONE

A FARMSTAY IN THE SUBURBS

Time and time again, whenever we announced a new project, we'd get bombarded with one impatient question: "Is it Erin's turn yet?"

As the operations director at Three Birds Renovations, Erin is all about perfect planning and meticulous detail, so finding the right home to renovate took time. With the big reveal of this Urban Farmhouse project, the wait is finally over – and boy, was it worth every second!

Erin had been dreaming of this reno for years. The house had great bones and the property itself was love at first sight, with its lush gardens, pool, cabana and even tennis court – talk about a bonus! But the house? Well, it needed a serious makeover to match modern lifestyles and bring it into the current century.

When Erin and Nathan bought the property, it was your typical 1990s brick-and-terracotta home. Its rectangular shape and gabled roof reminded Erin of a traditional farmhouse, so we leaned into that classic architectural style and used it as the foundation for this transformation. No frilly curtains or plaid here! Instead, we gave the home a facade makeover and injected warmth and texture into the dated interiors for the perfect blend of farmhouse charm with a modern urban twist.

From re-imagined open-plan living spaces to a show-stopping alfresco entertaining area, this renovation is easily one of our biggest and best yet. We give you the Urban Farmhouse of Erin's imagination.

AFTER

SAME SAME, BUT VERY DIFFERENT

It's always fun at the end of a reno to try to remember what things used to look like. That's why taking before and after pics is a must. Document the whole process and you'll be able to see how far the transformation has come. How many changes can you spot in this pic?

GOING GAGA FOR GABLES

Gabled roofs are a hallmark of farmhouse design, so we needed to embrace them in this renovation. To nail that authentic farmhouse vibe (and for a more practical entry point), we relocated the front door to the centre of the facade and added a gorgeous portico with another gable to highlight that classic look.

FROM BLAND TO GRAND

This was our biggest facade transformation yet! The Urban Farmhouse went from plain and forgettable to a total showstopper. We completely re-imagined the front, adding character and charm with new cladding, steel roofing, fresh paint and sophisticated black window frames. Girlfriend got a glow-up!

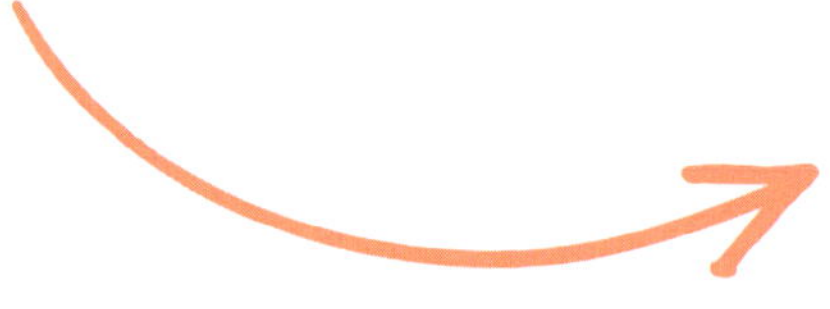

FARMHOUSE FACADE FACELIFT

When we say total facade transformation, we mean the whole shebang! We kept a touch of brick for nostalgia, but everything else got an overhaul. Here's how we brought this Urban Farmhouse dream facade to life.

1. **Roof:** This house has a lot of roof, and because it sits downhill from the road, you can see almost every inch. We swapped the dated terracotta tiles for steel panels in a deep, cool grey colour.
2. **Exterior walls:** We went all out on texture! We painted parts of the original brick and added vertical cladding and stonewalling for timeless charm.
3. **Windows:** Black window frames were non-negotiable in Erin's vision. We used commercial-grade aluminium which is super sleek and low-maintenance.
4. **Colour:** To tie it all together, Dulux "Grey Port" was our colour of choice on both the cladding and the brick, creating a cohesive look.

RENO SCHOOL TOP TIP

With any renovation, identifying and embracing the architectural style of your existing home will make life much easier – and will make creating a vision board a breeze. Turning an Art Deco home into a Mediterranean casa or a contemporary home into a farmhouse will require a much larger and more costly transformation than working with the bones of what you already have.

AFTER

CURVED COUCH MAGIC

The gorgeous bouclé sofa is a perfect fit for an open-plan living area. Its soft curves give the illusion of more space to move around in, helping to define the living zone without overwhelming it. It's comfy enough for lounging, yet light enough not to dominate the room.

DEFINE YOUR VISION TO AVOID CLICHÉS

A clear vision is essential for styling your lounge in a way that feels authentic and avoids design clichés. For this renovation, we embraced an Urban Farmhouse aesthetic – a blend of timeless charm and modern practicality, ideal for a busy family home. This vision guided our choices for soft furnishings, allowing us to create a space that felt warm and inviting without overdoing the farmhouse look. The result? Beautiful, functional pieces that captured the style without veering into overly rustic or outdated territory.

SAVVY SAVER

See those stunning doors? They may look like steel, but they're actually timber, painted black! A clever hack for getting that high-end steel look without the price tag.

LET YOUR PANTRY SHINE

When your butler's pantry looks just as lovely as your kitchen, why not let it shine? Adding glass doors can make it feel like part of the design story. With an abundance of shelving, beautiful cabinetry and thoughtful styling, it becomes both practical and stylish. Whether you're prepping meals or grabbing a quick snack, this space adds a little extra charm to everyday life.

WHERE CANVAS MEETS CANNED GOODS

Why should your pantry miss out on the fun? Adding art instantly elevates the space and sparks joy – even when you're just grabbing a tin of tomatoes!

SHELF-ISH DELIGHT

Just because it's a practical space doesn't mean it can't be pretty as a picture. In your butler's pantry, style your shelves to showcase your best pieces and add a touch of charm. Whether it's your favourite ceramics, your glassware or pantry essentials in beautiful jars, these little details can make all the difference. A few well-placed items will elevate the space, making it feel just as special as the rest of your home.

FARMHOUSE FLAIR MEETS URBAN CHIC

These five features make up the heart and soul of the Urban Farmhouse kitchen.

- ✓ **Warm, natural materials:** The light wood cabinetry and marble-look surfaces create a cosy, inviting vibe that's both modern and timeless.
- ✓ **Seamless butler's pantry:** The open access to the butler's pantry keeps everything within reach and maintains the kitchen's clean, uncluttered look.
- ✓ **Airy and open design:** The many windows, light palette and minimalist layout make the space feel bright, open and perfect for family gatherings.
- ✓ **Functional island with seating:** The island offers ample workspace and seating, making it the perfect spot for casual meals or socialising while cooking.
- ✓ **Simple styling:** Simple, rustic decor pieces add personality and warmth without overwhelming the space, keeping the farmhouse style elegant and fresh.

COUNTRY KITCHEN REVIVAL

Talk about a comeback! This dated suburban kitchen has been transformed into a fresh and modern Urban Farmhouse dream. With pale timber tones, open shelving and a stunning island bench, it's now the heart of the home.

BENCHMARK BEAUTY

The showstopper in this kitchen? The huge island bench. And just look at the chunk on it! We used the same stone for the benchtops, the splashback, the bold apron detail and the sleek kickboards. The island is a centrepiece that adds both style and substance to the space.

LET'S SPICE THINGS UP

This cleverly recessed spice rack pulls out when you're ready to season your dishes at the stove and tucks away seamlessly when you're done. It's a smart use of the unused cavity space behind the fridge.

GOOD THINGS COME IN THREES

When it comes to styling, the rule of threes is your secret weapon. Grouping items in threes creates a sense of balance and visual interest that's pleasing to the eye. Whether it's a cluster of three objects like we've used here, a trio of cushions on the couch or a set of three wall prints, odd numbers create a dynamic look. It's an easy way to add that perfectly curated feel to any space – because good things really do come in threes!

Where inside meets outside in the most delicious way.

SEAT YOURSELF

Erin says...

"I love to entertain friends and family, so plenty of seating was a must (Bonnie might say *too much* seating!). I wanted stools at the island bench, more at the servery and a full dining set-up to fit as many bottoms as possible. The best part about styling your own home is that you get to do it in a way that suits you!"

Save the standout
This original sunroom was too good to let go, so we built the magic around it.

THE WONDER OF WASHABLE COVERS

Who will be eating at your place – do you need something kid-friendly and easy to clean? These comfy chairs come with washable covers – win-win!

GIRLS AND GLASS CEILINGS

This is one glass ceiling we definitely didn't want to smash! We were given the fabulous focal feature of a glass atrium with the original home, and we couldn't have built it better ourselves if we'd tried.

If your home has an existing feature like this, lucky you! Add it to your "keep" list quick smart and plan how to revive it rather than remove it during your renovation.

A CHAIR AFFAIR

The first thing to consider when picking dining chairs is how many people you need to seat around your table. This will help you decide whether you can opt for big, comfy chairs with arms or if you need to be more space-savvy – maybe even consider a bench if you have a rectangular table. What's your magic number?

SAVVY SAVER

Why break the bank with a cabinet-maker when you can have your chippie work wonders instead? Fibre cement cladding is not just weatherproof but also perfect for building outdoor kitchens that are both durable and budget-friendly. Your builder or carpenter can frame up the bench, line it with fibre cement sheets, and cut out the doors. Finish it off with a benchtop and handles of your choice. Now that's a recipe for success!

ALL HAIL THE AUTOMATED AWNINGS

A shout-out to the heroes of this space – the automated awnings. We've used them before, and we'll use them again and again for their ability to weatherproof outdoor areas, allowing you to enjoy alfresco dining no matter the weather. Plus, they're motorised and retract completely out of sight with the touch of a button.

DESK WITH A VIEW

TABLE TALK

Who says your home office needs a traditional desk? We say ditch the desk and opt for a gorgeous table instead. A table creates a more open, airy feel than a bulky desk, giving your home office a designer touch with room to spread out and get creative. Work smarter, and definitely more stylishly!

CENTRE STAGE

Lana recommends...

"Placing your desk in the centre of the room creates such an open, inviting vibe. You get a view of the good stuff, and suddenly your workday feels less like a chore and more like a luxe experience. I've done this in my own home office, and let me tell you – it's so much more inspiring than staring at a wall all day!"

Tonal texture is the trick! Layer similar shades in different fabrics for a look that's calm, collected and never boring.

A little light goes a long way – perfect for reading in your cosy window seat nook.

MAKE YOUR STUDY WORK OVERTIME

Why settle for a single-purpose room when your study can work overtime? This space was designed with flexibility in mind – it can easily transform into a fifth bedroom if needed. With a built-in wardrobe, a stylish window seat, an ensuite and external access, it's perfect for an older child or guest to stay comfortably. Now that's smart design!

TURN UP THE TEXTURE

Your walls don't all have to be plain plasterboard. You can add texture to your walls by incorporating trims like these timber mouldings in the living room above which we've extended across the ceiling too. This room wouldn't feel nearly as inviting without them – they not only add depth but also help highlight features like the artwork.

LANDING LOVE

Turn your landing into a luxe moment: add a statement chair, a floor lamp and a rug to make it feel like a purposeful, inviting space.

RENO SCHOOL INSIGHT

Install your washing machine and dryer off the floor to make loading and unloading a breeze. No more back strain! And add a handy pull-out shelf below each appliance for your laundry basket. But just make sure the machines are safely secured inside the cabinetry so they can't wriggle out!

WASH DAY DELIGHTS

These delightful additions to the Urban Farmhouse laundry will make washing a joy.

- ✓ Hanging rails for drying shirts and delicates
- ✓ A window for natural ventilation
- ✓ Plenty of bench space for folding
- ✓ Farmhouse-feel tiles
- ✓ Fresh foliage in a vase

Function meets fabulous
Turn a vanity into a design moment with a sculptural basin.

SOAK IT UP

Don't put your loo on view – the first thing you should see when you walk into a bathroom is a beautiful set-up like this. Here's the formula for a spa-worthy vibe.

- ✓ Free-standing bath under the window
- ✓ Sculpture-like bath tap
- ✓ Shelf for your soaps and scrubs
- ✓ Stool for your towel (and glass of vino)

KISS

Sometimes simplicity is the best design choice. When your basin is the hero, why complicate things with a fussy vanity? Keep it simple, sweetie. (PS There's storage behind the mirror.)

SAVVY SAVER

Modern laminate can now mimic real marble, offering all the elegance without the hefty price tag. We used it on the vanity and splashback in this powder room with stunning results. Plus, it's super lightweight, making installation an absolute breeze. Stylish, affordable and easy – what's not to love?

Pro tip from our cabinet-maker: choose "post-formed" laminate to wrap around benchtop edges for a high-end seamless look without visible joins.

HOW'S THE SERENITY?

The key to this serene space is the subtle repetition of soft, rounded edges to offset all the angles. Spot the curves on the sink, the mirror, the tapware, the wall sconce, the bath and even the hand wash.

CREAMY DREAMY DELIGHT

Let's talk colour palette. In this bathroom, it's all about soft neutrals – warm creams and light, earthy tones that create a calm, inviting space. These neutral hues bring a timeless elegance, allowing the textures and finishes, like the tiles and tapware, to take centre stage.

TACTILE, TONAL DREAM.

Double duty desk
Study desk or glam station?

PAD IT OUT

For a touch of luxury and comfort in a teen girl's bedroom, an upholstered bedhead in plush velvet is an absolute winner. It creates a cosy, inviting feel while adding a layer of softness and sophistication to the room. Perfect for leaning back against while lounging, reading or scrolling, this padded beauty is a statement piece that brings both style and comfort to any dreamy teen retreat.

Kids' rooms are the perfect place to dial up the fun with colour and pattern.

ENSUITE ENVY

We know an ensuite isn't usually a standard feature in a kid's bedroom – and it wasn't even planned for this house. But lucky for this little lady, her bedroom had an unused study nook just begging to be transformed into an ensuite. Now she's got her own personal bathroom, and the rest of us are feeling some serious ensuite envy!

SCONCE SENSE

Ditch the bedside lamps and go for wall sconces instead! Mounting sconces beside the bed frees up valuable space on your bedside tables, giving you more room for books and whatever other essentials you like to keep close by.

Skip the bedhead
Centre the bed under the window for maximum light.

DARE TO BE BOLD?

Bedrooms offer an opportunity to play with colour. We painted this one in a deep, striking blue that adds depth and dimension. You might remember this shade from the boys' bedroom in our Australian Staycation build (as seen in our second book). Even after sampling other blues, Bonnie knew this one was a winner. When you find something that works, stick with it!

DESK-OVER UNUSED SPACES

Every nook and cranny is an opportunity to add function and style! Take a cue from this set-up, where we've custom-built a desk to fit perfectly into the space. It's a clever way to make the most of those tricky spots while adding purpose to the room.

Mirrors expand and brighten every space, bringing sparkle.

ERIN'S WIR STYLE CHECKLIST

These three small details have a big impact.

- ✓ **Linen-look cabinetry:** It may look like delicate linen, but it's actually a durable Polytec finish that's resistant to marks.
- ✓ **Carpet:** But make it bouclé! Not only is it cosy underfoot, but it also brings a touch of elegance to the space.
- ✓ **The perfect balance of pretty and practical:** Find the sweet spot between hanging space, drawers, open shelves and closed storage. Add some beautiful display shelving to elevate the room and make it feel extra special.

These boots are made for walk-in!

PLAN THE POWER POINTS!

When designing your walk-in robe, don't forget about the power points. You'll thank yourself later for placing them in smart spots for charging your phone, heating your hair straightener or powering your steamer. Think about where you'll need them most – like near mirrors for hair tools or by shelving for those must-have gadgets. It's all about making your walk-in robe not just stylish, but super functional too.

A POP OF PEACHY FUN.

A LITTLE BIT CHEEKY

Your bedroom, your rules, we say! The art you choose for this room is for your eyes only, so anything goes. The colours of this Slim Aarons print complement the colour palette and theme of the room perfectly.

LOUIS VUITTON

URBAN FARMHOUSE MAIN BEDROOM HONOUR ROLL

- ✓ **The colour palette:** Since this room is blessed with plenty of natural light, we chose the full-strength version of the colour used throughout the rest of the house for the walls, trims and ceiling. It's glowy, cosy and sophisticated.
- ✓ **Wall detailing:** Skirting and architraves can make or break a room. In Erin's bedroom, the 300 mm skirting, paired with decorative architraves and vertical cladding, elevates the luxe factor.
- ✓ **Luxe furnishings and bedding:** The beautiful bed is the centrepiece of this space. We paired it with matching side tables, bedside lamps and French linen bedding for the ultimate luxurious finish.

GET THE SHOWER HEIGHT RIGHT

Aim for a shower head height between 2000 and 2200 mm. Our trick? Get a tall tradie to stand in the shower while marking it out with the plumber. Don't go too high, though – shorter people need it to be practical too. That's why adjustable rail showers are a lifesaver for everyone in the family.

SLIDE INTO PRIVACY

We know open ensuites are all the rage, but if you're someone who values a bit more privacy, a cavity slider door is the perfect solution. It slides away completely flush, so when it's open, it's invisible – but when you need a little "me" time, it gives you privacy without compromising on style. Best of both worlds!

REFRESH YOUR BEST ASSETS

This property already had a pool, but it needed a little TLC to get it back to its best. We emptied it, gave it a deep clean and replaced the waterline tiles and surrounding pavers. Now it looks as good as new!

PULL UP A PAIR AND ENJOY THE VIEW

Placing a pair of stylish chairs where you have a view worth admiring – whether it's of a sparkling pool or a beautiful atrium – creates the perfect spot to sit and soak it all in.

BABY GOT BACK!

Who doesn't love a good rear view? Your backyard, rear exterior and outdoor entertaining spaces deserve just as much attention as the front. Whether it's installing doors for that seamless indoor–outdoor flow, creating a dreamy alfresco dining area or giving your garden a refresh, give the back of your home some love – it's where the real fun happens.

PUNCH OUT THE PORCH

At this house, the existing back porch was far too small for the property, so extending it was a must. It ended up being the biggest structural part of the renovation. We more than doubled the depth of the original porch, creating a 5.5 x 12-metre entertaining area with plenty of room for lounging and dining, and even its own kitchen. Now it's the ultimate outdoor space, perfect for enjoying the good life.

MODERN MALLORCA

A MEDITERRANEAN HOLIDAY AT HOME

CHAPTER TWO

A MEDITERRANEAN HOLIDAY AT HOME

Nestled in sunny Sydney, this three-storey beauty came with a touch of Mediterranean flair already in place – think architectural arches, a wrought iron balustrade and sweeping water views 🤌!

But here's the catch – the floor plan was a disaster: a rabbit warren of odd-shaped rooms, dark and unwelcoming spaces, mismatched styles and different floor heights. It was anything but functional.

The brief? Simple in theory, but far from easy in execution. We needed to create a beautiful, functional home that was perfect for family life and working from home, yet also ready to entertain guests and welcome the occasional overseas visitor. So, our mission was clear: transform this jumbled property into a seamless, inviting family haven with an effortless flow and those Mediterranean-inspired vibes we all adore.

We knocked down walls to open up the layout and let the sunshine pour in, flooding every room with natural light to create that bright, open-plan flow we love. The once dark, disconnected spaces are now airy, light-filled living areas. Every inch of this home was crafted to make it feel like a Mediterranean retreat.

The result? A modern Mallorcan masterpiece. The lucky owners can now live their best island-holiday life every single day – right at home. From the open, breezy spaces to the charming details, this home is now a dreamy slice of Spain in the heart of Sydney. *Salud* to that!

ARCH ARCH, BABY!

The existing arches were the starting point for this Mediterranean-inspired vision. Coated in creamy, undulating render and paired with stone cladding, they blur the boundaries between indoors and outdoors. Arches are a surefire way to give your property that unmistakable Mediterranean vibe.

JUST ADD WATER

An island-inspired vision calls for water views, and this house ticks that box with jaw-dropping outlooks that instantly transport you to the coast. But don't worry if your home doesn't come with those views, because there's a clever way to fake it till you make it: a swimming pool! Adding a pool not only brings those calming island vibes to your backyard, but it also creates the perfect focal point for outdoor entertaining. Pro tip: Keep the area around your pool light and breezy with neutral tones, lush greenery and plenty of space to lounge – it'll make every day feel like a holiday at home.

POOL ROOM BY DAY, GUEST ROOM BY NIGHT

Why let a guest room sit empty most of the year when you can create a space that does double duty? In this home, we needed a place for overseas relatives to stay for weeks at a time. But instead of dedicating an entire room that would gather dust when guests weren't around, we designed a multi-functional space to be enjoyed year-round. By day, it's a stylish pool room – perfect for lounging by the water, entertaining or simply unwinding. And when guests come to stay, it easily transforms into a cosy, welcoming guest room.

HALLMARKS OF THIS MODERN MALLORCA CASA

The essentials for creating this slice of Spain in Sydney:

- ✓ **arches:** the more the better
- ✓ **textured render:** for that authentic Mediterranean vibe
- ✓ **stone cladding:** for that "been here forever" feel #Palma
- ✓ **warm creamy white paint:** Dulux "White Dune Quarter"
- ✓ **pops of Mediterranean bluey green:** "Dulux Coalition".

Black pops perfectly in calm, neutral spaces.

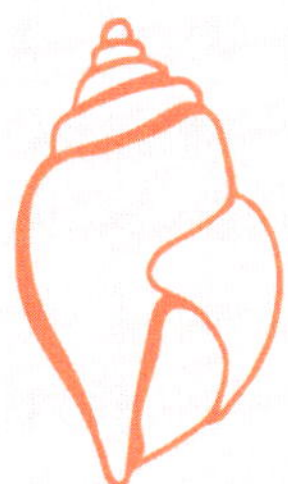

MAKE ROOM FOR APERITIVOS

Why head out for a drink when you can bring the bar home? Adding a built-in bar to your entertaining space is a fabulous way to create that holiday-at-home vibe. A dedicated nook with elegant shelving and plenty of space for glassware sets the scene perfectly for aperitivos with friends or a cosy nightcap. Cheers!

RENO SCHOOL TOP TIP

Repeat after us: "When it comes to great design, repetition is your best friend." Repeating shapes, colours or materials throughout your home creates a sense of cohesion and flow that's easy on the eye. You can see how we've done it here: using the same wave motif on the vanity as in other rooms, the same tiles as other bathrooms (though laid differently), and a fluted glass shower screen like in the ensuite. Repetition doesn't mean boring – it's about creating rhythm and harmony so that all the corners of your home feel connected.

MULTI-PURPOSE = MUY BUENO!

Your entry foyer can be more than just a spot to drop your keys. Here, we took multi-purpose living to the next level by combining the entry foyer with a guest room, ensuite, lounge, bar and even a mudroom.

STAR OF THE SHOW

Erin says...

"For me, practicality is always key, and the best feature of this space is the ability to close off the bedroom and bathroom to give guests their privacy. The star of the show? The motorised dividing curtain. When not in use, it disappears into a recessed cavity like it was never there. We chose a fabric that is opaque enough for privacy but still lets in a soft, warm glow – and she absolutely shines."

GUESS WHERE THE GUESTS SLEEP?

Forget the standard bed frame. For this guest room, we went all out with a custom-built, curvy rendered surround for the bed. It's a stylish showstopper that doubles as a stunning daybed when the space isn't being used for overnight guests, combining form and function for a space that works hard year-round.

The real genius? A high-quality mattress that guarantees your guests a dreamy night's sleep, making them feel like they're staying at a luxury resort.

SUPER-SIZE ME

When it comes to making a statement, bigger is definitely better – especially with your front door. Oversized doors not only add a dramatic touch but also create a grand, welcoming entrance that instantly elevates your space. They also bring in more natural light, enhance airflow and blur the lines between indoor and outdoor living. Oh, and you'll thank us when that huge sofa you bought has to come through the front door.

MAKE A STATEMENT WITH A SCULPTURAL STAIRCASE

A staircase doesn't have to be just functional – it can be a stunning focal point too. A sculptural staircase adds an artistic, architectural element to your home. It's not just about getting from A to B; it's about making a statement while you do it.

TAKE A PEEK AT THE PIVOT DOOR

Elevate your front door game with a pivot door! Unlike traditional swing doors, pivot doors hinge from the top and bottom, delivering a sleek, seamless look with serious architectural flair.

OPEN UP TO THE OUTDOORS

In Australia, making the most of our gorgeous climate is a must. And the best way to do that? Maximise your indoor–outdoor flow. Adding multiple access points to balconies and outdoor spaces can transform your home into a breezy oasis.

THE ONLY WAY IS UP

This home is spread over three levels, and the staircase is a unifying design feature that ties them all together. It offers this winning trifecta.

1. Rendered walls for that soft, textural feel.
2. A sleek black steel handrail for a sophisticated contrast.
3. Engineered timber stairs that bring warmth and natural beauty.

If you're after an effortless Mediterranean touch to your styling, olive trees are the way to go. Potted or planted, they're fabulous!

BALUSTRADE BEAUTY

Custom balustrades are the perfect way to add character and elegance to your home, and we designed this steel one to reflect the curves and arches throughout the house. Don't underestimate the power of small design moments like this – they make all the difference!

SHADES OF SOPHISTICATION

Level up your lounge room with strategic pops of black. These striking accents – like the black coffee table, fireplace and even TV (which we don't usually like to highlight!) – create bold contrast against the warm whites and neutrals in the room. The black handrail on the stairs and the lamp on the console table tie it all together, adding an air of elegance that makes this space feel ultra-chic.

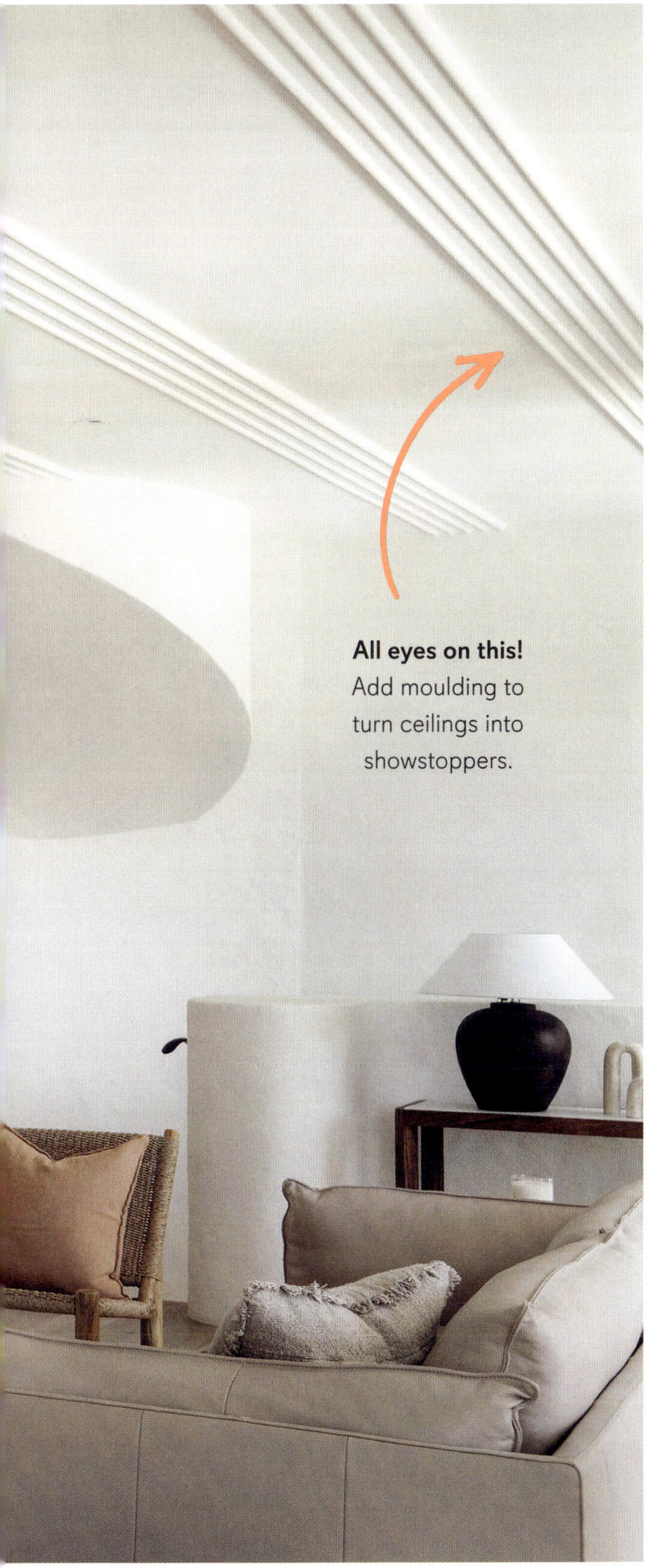

All eyes on this! Add moulding to turn ceilings into showstoppers.

CALM. CURVES. CHARACTER.

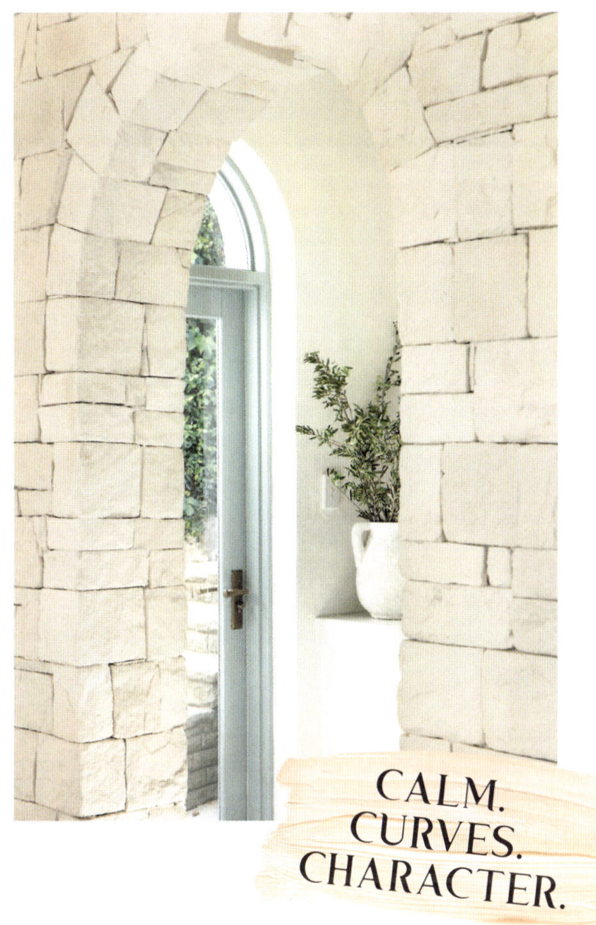

LAYER UP THE LUXE

We mixed textures to add warmth, sticking to a cosy colour palette with bouclé armchairs, a plush rug, and a marble and timber console. A touch of stone cladding brings natural elegance, and duck feather cushions add the final touch of perfection. Karate chop!

SET THE TONE WITH TEXTURE

When creating a #ModernMallorca vibe, texture is key, and nothing does it better than beautiful stone cladding. The stone feature wall in this lounge room deserves a special mention – it sets the tone for the entire home with its natural rustic charm.

Sconce and sensibility
Small light, big
luxe vibes.

SAVVY SAVER

Stone cladding gives you the look and feel of real stone without the complexity – it's made from a blend of crushed sandstone and comes in easy-to-handle tiles which are cheaper to install than the real deal. Whether inside or out (we've done both at this house), it's a stunning way to bring texture, warmth and character to any space.

OPEN DOOR POLICY

Does a butler's pantry need a door? That's totally up to you. If you prefer to keep things hidden away, a door will be your best ally in maintaining a clean, streamlined look. But if you love the idea of easy access and keeping the flow open, go without. It all comes down to how you use the space and the vibe you want to create.

EURO LAUNDRY – SMALL SPACE, BIG IMPACT

When we're designing a Euro-inspired home, a Euro laundry is a no-brainer. Euro house, Euro laundry – it just fits! Tucked neatly behind bi-fold doors or hidden within cabinetry, it makes every centimetre count. Thanks to its smart storage and compact appliances, you get a streamlined, efficient laundry zone that's both stylish and super functional – perfect for modern living.

Hide and sleek
Integrated appliance = all the function, none of the fuss.

BULLNOSE EDGING IS BACK IN BUSINESS!

POLISHED OR MATTE? MAKE YOUR STONE SHINE

This stunning benchtop stone, with its deep white base and delicate gold veins, brings both lightness and warmth to the room. We opted for a polished finish, which creates a gorgeous contrast against the matte stone cladding feature wall – we love a bit of texture play! The result? An island bench that steals the spotlight, giving the whole space a sophisticated blend of shine and subtlety.

A statement cooker can anchor your entire kitchen design. Build your cabinetry, colours and hardware around it to create a focal point.

COOKER + RANGE HOOD = PERFECT PAIR

A perfectly matched cooker and range hood pair can be the hero of your kitchen, adding both style and substance to your cooking space.

INTEGRATE – OR HIDE – THE APPLIANCES

Let's be honest, integrating your kitchen appliances is a real luxury, not something that every kitchen budget allows. But when it's possible, we love how an integrated fridge can create a stunning, seamless and symmetrical look for your kitchen. If full integration isn't within your budget, don't worry. You can still achieve a tidy hidden-appliance vibe with clever solutions like pocket doors to keep things out of sight when not in use. It's all about smart design, no matter the budget.

THE BULLNOSE IS BACK, BABY!

Say hello to the return of the chunky bullnose! This bold profile on your kitchen benchtop adds a touch of nostalgia with a modern twist. Not only does it bring soft, rounded edges that are easy on the eye, but it also creates a sense of solid luxury. Measuring 2.95 x 1.3 metres with a 100 mm bullnose profile, it's not the largest island we've ever done, but it's definitely the chunkiest.

"COALITION"
BY DULUX

ENHANCE THE BEST ELEMENTS

If you've got a stunning view, why not frame it like a piece of art with an arched window?

GREEN OR GREY? OR BLUE?

Throughout this renovation there was hot debate on the building site about the best way to describe the accent colour we chose for the window frames. Is it green? Is it grey, or even blue? The colour is "Coalition" by Dulux. You decide and let us know!

SAY YES TO FUN UPHOLSTERY

Why play it safe when you can have fun with your furniture? Say yes to bold, playful upholstery! Whether it's a curved edge, a pop of colour, a fun fabric or a lush texture, your upholstery is the perfect way to inject personality into any room. It's a simple way to make a statement, spark joy and bring a fun, fresh vibe to your space.

MAKING WAVES

To create a dreamy bench seat backrest, make a wave (or any shape you fancy) by drawing a template on cardboard for your upholsterer to follow. A wavy silhouette can transform an ordinary back cushion into a unique design feature.

I SPY CONSISTENCY FROM THE OUTSIDE IN

Take a sneak peek from the undercover balcony into the dining room, thanks to perfectly framed windows and doors. We used the muted blue-green shade to tie the inside and outside spaces together. The soft, calming tone adds a subtle touch of colour while seamlessly connecting the two areas.

WINDOW OF OPPORTUNITY

It might be tempting to think that more glass must be better – but that's not always the case. If you're trying to create a timeless, "built long ago" feel, it's all about framing the view, not just exposing it.

In this case, smaller arched windows enhance the feeling of looking out to sea in the Mediterranean, giving this home the nostalgic character we were after. Adding a cosy bench seat beneath the window brings extra charm and connects perfectly with our vision board for this home.

AFTER

NOT YOUR AVERAGE STUDY DESK

Never settle for ordinary when you can create something extraordinary. We turned a simple study desk into a statement piece by curving the edges and crafting decorative legs using timber mouldings. This special touch makes the desk a standout feature in the room.

GLASS DOORS FOR THE WIN

We love a home office that's bathed in natural light and feels connected to the rest of the home, and glass doors are the perfect way to achieve that. They let the light flow through and keep you feeling part of the action while you're working. But when it's time to focus and get down to business (hello, Zoom calls), you can simply close them for some peace and quiet. It's truly the best of both worlds.

RENO SCHOOL TOP TIP

Make the most of the space in a small powder room by opting for a wall-hung basin instead of a bulky vanity. It keeps the floor area open, making the room feel bigger and less cluttered. And for storing those essentials? Hide a slim cupboard behind the mirror – it's the perfect spot to stash an extra roll of loo paper without sacrificing style.

SNEAKY SLIDER HERE.

Add timber mouldings for subtle curves and serious style points.

CUTIE-PIE POWDER ROOM ENTRY

Step through a teeny tiny arched door and you'll find our cutie-pie powder room! This adorable entrance was a compromise we made so we could make the statement staircase as wide as possible. Do we regret it? Not one bit! Although it's narrower than standard, this arched doorway adds a playful architectural detail that sets the tone for the entire space. The soft curves of the arch create a whimsical vibe, making every trip to the powder room feel like a special experience. It's proof that even the smallest doors can make the biggest impact.

Stool or table? Entertain with flexible style.

FROM GLOOMY TO VA-VA-VOOMY!

Transforming a tired outdoor area into a vibrant Mediterranean courtyard is easier than you think.

1. Start by adding textured white walls or stone cladding for that sun-soaked rustic vibe.
2. Layer in a tiled floor with a fun pattern to inject some colour, and don't forget to add a built-in kitchen with a barbecue and a fridge to keep the drinks cold and the crowds fed.
3. Finish off with plenty of seating (built-in bench seats are always a winner) and an umbrella for shade, and voilà – you've got yourself a Mediterranean escape right in your backyard!

SUNNY SIDE UP

When the wind's kicking up out front, this cute little courtyard is the perfect retreat. Protected from the breeze and a gorgeous sun trap, especially in the afternoons, it's the ideal spot to soak up some rays and relax in total peace.

CHECKMATE

Here's a winning move: we laid the same tiles inside and out for a seamless flow that blurs the lines between indoor and outdoor living. It's checkmate when it comes to creating a cohesive, stylish look that feels spacious and connected. Plus, it's super practical for entertaining, with no awkward transitions – just one beautiful, uninterrupted surface.

BEYOND PIZZA

Did you know that pizza ovens aren't just for pizza? Think wood-fired fish, charred vegies, crusty bread or even toasted marshmallows. The possibilities are endless, and they'll all add a delicious twist to your alfresco gatherings.

ROUND IT OUT

A round table in the centre of the room creates an open and inviting vibe, and it also allows for better flow throughout the space. Plus, with no sharp corners, it's perfect for collaborative sessions or when you just want to spread out and get creative.

BATHROOM BEAUTY FIRST

When you step into a bathroom, you want to be greeted by something beautiful – like a stunning freestanding bath and a gorgeous view, right? That's why we've tucked the loo out of sight. It's all about making first impressions count.

ADD A SHOWER SHELF (OR SEAT!)

The shower shelf we built looks like it's been here for hundreds of years, thanks to the textured finish and rounded edges.

CHECK THIS OUT

For a bold yet timeless look, try a checkerboard lay for your bathroom tiles. Use four squares of one colour and four squares of another to create an oversized checkerboard effect.

THE TIDAL WAVE EFFECT

Consistency is everything when it comes to nailing a cohesive look. In this bathroom, we've carried the wave design from other parts of the house into the vanity cabinetry, creating a seamless flow. Remember, repeating key design elements – such as patterns, textures, colours or shapes – throughout your home makes every room feel connected and intentional.

SAVVY SAVER

Most parents buy each kid a standard single bed after they've outgrown their cot, but this usually means yet another bed purchase down the track as your toddler grows into a teenager. We say skip the standard single and go straight for a king single or double (or bigger!) – it'll save you an upgrade later.

Go big or go home: bed edition Upsize the doona for an extra-cosy overhang!

Arched nook magic The perfect little perch for your precious pieces.

Around the bend Yes, curved skirting is a thing! Bring those luscious curved walls into your life wherever possible.

SCALLOP SPOTTO

Did you spot the gorgeous bed frame (and rug) with the beautiful scalloped detailing? It repeats the wave/scallop motif used throughout the house, tying the design together for a cohesive and harmonious look.

NICHE KNOWLEDGE

Creating a niche for storage in a bedroom is a brilliant way to maximise space and showcase some decor. And the best bit? You can have one in your home too! Behind most walls sits a cavity, thanks to the framework. It's these cavities, in between the timbers, that are perfect for carving out your niche. Just don't go niche crazy – you can have too many niches! Or can you?

SUNSHINE, RAINBOWS & LOLLIPOPS

Children's bedrooms should spark joy, and bed linen is a fabulous way to bring in the fun. For this tween girl's room, we went with a luscious colour palette in checks and stripes, creating a bedding combo that's almost good enough to eat.

LUXE WARDROBES FOR LESS

We gave these wardrobe doors a high-end look by adding half-round mouldings and travertine arched handles. Painted to match the window frames, they're now full of curves, charm and luxe – without the luxe price tag.

PITCH PERFECT

If you're blessed with a pitched ceiling, it's definitely worth making a fuss over! We accentuated the shape of this ceiling by adding feature beams and painted it a delicious custard yellow (Dulux "Curd Half") to really make it pop. The result? A dramatic focal point that adds height, character and a whole lot of wow factor to the room.

BESIDE THE BED

In small bedrooms, you might be better off with just one bedside table. If you love the classic symmetrical look, by all means go for a matching set. But if you're all about that eclectic vibe and you laugh in the face of symmetry, mix it up!

DULUX
"CURD HALF"

What girl wouldn't want her very own daybed in her bedroom?

TIME TO UNWIND

A luxe parents' retreat? Absolutely non-negotiable for any high-end home with "vacay vibes"! It's the ultimate sanctuary – a private little slice of heaven in your home where you can kick back, recharge and escape the beautiful chaos of family life.

Spot the cutesy built-in dressing table through the arched entrance.

PARED BACK & PEACEFUL

Bonnie says...

"Inspired by my travels to Mallorca and the authentic way that hotels there style bedrooms, I skipped the mountain of decorative cushions and went for a pared-back, peaceful look. No Euro cushions in this Euro-inspired space – oh, the irony! Less is definitely more here."

A ROOM WITH A VIEW

The arched window in this parents' retreat is all about making a statement: it frames the gorgeous view like a piece of art. To make it even better, we added a custom cushion with plush upholstery, creating the perfect perch to sit back, relax and soak it all in. This dreamy little space blends comfort with luxury, making every moment spent here feel extra special.

ACCESS ALL AREAS

It seemed a crime not to be able to access the outdoors from this top level of the home, so a top-level balcony was a key part of the renovation plans. Check out the super cute arched detail we added to the glass doors. They create an arch when the doors are closed. It's little touches like this that take a home to the next level.

This statement bed base is the perfect foundation for a laid-back vibe. Sweet dreams guaranteed!

Sculptural shapes steal the show in this serene ensuite.

DUAL VANITIES

Say goodbye to bathroom battles by creating two separate vanities! They do more than add a touch of luxury – they create personal spaces so everyone can get ready in peace, with no elbowing for counter space. Functional, stylish and a total game-changer for harmonious mornings.

BATHING WITH A VIEW

No need to waste the best view on the loo! We saved the prime spot in the room for the bath, so the bather can relax in style.

WINE GLASS
GOES HERE.

COASTAL DREAM

OUR SIGNATURE STYLE

CHAPTER THREE

OUR SIGNATURE STYLE

Your coastal holiday at home starts right here.

Many moons ago, we had the wild idea of building a project home so beautiful, you'd swear it was custom-built.

Fast-forward a few years and that dream came true! We teamed up with a project home company to carefully craft our Coastal Dream, poring over every detail from our past projects and pulling together all the must-have design features we've loved along the way.

We took a deep dive into every image and every room of our previous homes and cherry-picked the absolute best of the best to create a home that exudes our signature coastal cool style with that airy, light-filled vibe we can't get enough of. You might say it's the "best of the Birds".

Even though it's a project home, we hand-selected every single fixture and fitting – yes, down to the skirting boards, stair nosing and wall sconces. We left no stone unturned to ensure this house is a dreamy exemplar of breezy open-plan living, featuring our favourite elements: a white weatherboard exterior, engineered timber floors throughout the interior, and of course our signature gas-strut windows.
It's the ultimate family entertainer, designed for that seamless indoor–outdoor lifestyle we love.

Step inside our holiday at home...

67

ARE YOU A NERVOUS NEWBIE?

If you're a first-time builder, a project home might be the perfect place to start. You can try before you buy by walking through a display home, which will give you a clear idea of what to expect from the final build. There are some stunning project homes available that you can customise to make them feel uniquely yours.

COASTAL CHARM, ZERO FUSS

Worried about the upkeep of traditional timber weatherboards? Meet fibre cement, your coastal lifesaver. It's durable, it won't warp or swell, it resists moisture and termites, and it needs way less painting than timber boards. All the charm, none of the hassle!

SAVVY SAVER

On a budget? A project home might be your perfect match! With standardised designs and streamlined processes, they offer savings of thousands of dollars on a custom build. Plus, many builders offer flexible packages so you can upgrade finishes or add your personal touches without breaking the bank. The result? A stylish home minus the custom price tag.

GATE GOALS

Peekaboo! Your gates (and that first glimpse through them) set the scene for what's to come inside. Don't let your front yard be the forgotten sibling in your landscaping plans. Start strong with lush green turf, a charming stepping stone path and some established palm trees. Your front yard is the opening act to your home's vibe, so give it some love and make it a showstopper.

FULL FRONTAL

You've heard it before: first impressions count! Here's how to nail kerb appeal in coastal cool style.

- ✓ **Arched entry gate:** A simple yet striking detail that oozes classic charm.
- ✓ **Stone cladding:** Adds texture and warmth, grounding all that white with earthy, natural vibes.
- ✓ **Automated gate:** Timeless style meets modern convenience.
- ✓ **Palm trees:** Nothing says "coastal cool" quite like swaying palms.
- ✓ **White weatherboard:** The quintessential coastal exterior that's fresh and timeless.
- ✓ **Double French doors:** Elegant and inviting, perfect for creating that breezy indoor-outdoor flow.
- ✓ **White balustrade:** A crisp, clean finish that brings classic charm to your facade.

Together, these features create a welcoming vibe that's instantly inviting. Moral of the story? Don't skimp on your front fence – it's the front-row feature that sets the tone for your entire home.

WELCOME HOME WITH WEATHERBOARD

Bonnie says...

"In my mind, nothing says 'coastal charm' quite like a white weatherboard exterior. I used it on my own home (featured in our first book), which wasn't anywhere near the coast but still brought that dreamy vibe to our semi-rural property. For our Coastal Dream home, choosing a white weatherboard exterior was a total no-brainer – it's classic, timeless and oozes that laid-back coastal feel we love so much."

Can you spot all the circles and curves we repeated in this fire pit space? Even the sun hat plays its part ;-)

FIRE & FLAIR

Say bye-bye to basic backyard seating and create a dreamy little escape. A curved white bench and rattan chairs bring coastal charm, while a striped umbrella adds vacay vibes. Surround the fire pit with pebbles for a chic, low-maintenance "rug" that's perfect for sunset s'mores or Sunday morning coffees. Effortless style, sorted!

HONEY, I'M HOME!

Room to move – even cartwheel! That's exactly what we wanted for the entry of our Coastal Dream home. We prioritised an open, airy vibe from the moment you walk through the door, extending that feeling through the hallways and key areas of the house. It's all about creating an entrance you'll love coming home to, with plenty of room to breathe – gymnastics optional!

ADD A STAIRWAY TO HEAVEN

A staircase isn't just a functional fixture anymore – it's a design moment. If you want to create a grand entrance with serious wow factor, let your staircase steal the show.

SAY YES TO CURVES

From day one, we knew the staircase in our Coastal Dream home had to be more than just stairs – it had to be a moment. A statement. Something that would stop you in your tracks the first time you saw it. It's the star of the show the second you step inside, and honestly, one of our absolute fave features in the whole house. If your vision board says yes to curves, we say "Hell yeah!" – go for them wherever you can.

The round window centred over the laundry sink? A winning formula we'd happily use again and again.

Open shelves? Yes, please – but only for pretty stuff. Tuck the supermarket boxes and bottles away out of sight.

A DASH OF DEJA VU

Recognise this laundry? You're not imagining things – it's inspired by the Mediterranean Farmhouse home from our last book. We loved the layout so much, we had to include it in our Coastal Dream home. That's the beauty of home design: you don't need to reinvent the wheel every time. If you've spotted a design you adore on Pinterest or in a mag, copy it with pride! Just tweak the fittings and colours to suit your style.

SAVVY SAVER

Don't blow the budget on dining furniture. Splurge on a fabulous table and save on chairs, or vice versa. Mix, match and make it yours!

LOOKING FOR A GLAM GLOW-UP?

Want to add a little luxe to your laundry? Pop in a pendant light! It's the ultimate upgrade to take the space from "just functional" to "fabulous". Think of it as jewellery for your laundry – because even the hardest-working room deserves a touch of sparkle!

COLOUR ME PRETTY

If you're craving a pop of colour, the laundry is the perfect place to play. How about this gorgeous green? It's "Cat Mint" by Dulux, and it instantly elevates the mood.

Looking to add instant freshness to a space? Just add lemons... or anything citrus!

KEEP STYLING SIMPLE, SISTER!

Don't leave your table bare, but don't overcrowd it either. A couple of well-chosen centrepieces, like a vase, bowl or sculpture, are all you need. Bonus points for pieces you can easily move or leave in place during meals.

CREATE A SEAMLESS CONNECTION

Your alfresco area should feel like a natural extension of your indoor style – with outdoor-worthy materials. Bring your vibe to life outside by matching colour palettes, patterns, shapes and textures with what's happening indoors. A little matchy-matchy is a good thing here to nail that indoor–outdoor flow. #twinningiswinning

CUSHION COMFORT OUTDOORS

Outdoor cushions are the secret sauce to a cosy, stylish alfresco space. They add instant colour and comfort, but not all cushions are built for the outdoors. Look for weather-resistant fabrics that can handle the Aussie sun and rain. Removable, washable covers are best of all, so you can keep them fresh – then you'll have the ultimate year-round lounge spot.

Big vibes from the void Let the light flood in and your ceilings soar! Voids create instant drama, openness and allll the natural glow.

NO CORDS, NO CHAOS.

Serene green A living wall outdoors and pops of foliage inside combine with candles to set the mood.

INTEGRATE THE ENTERTAINMENT

Let's be honest, the TV isn't our favourite styling item, but it's a must-have in most modern living rooms. Make sure it's positioned for prime viewing from the sofa (hello, Netflix marathons!) and plan ahead for cord concealment. No one wants messy cables stealing the spotlight.

THIS IS A GREAT ROOM!

We're not just blowing our own trumpet – this really is a great room! A "great room" combines open-plan lounge, dining and living areas, typically right next to the kitchen, so the whole family can hang out together (but in their own zones). It's casual, functional and designed for everyday use – exactly what we had in mind for this space!

GAS STRUT GOALS.

DOUBLE HEIGHT, DOUBLE LIGHT

Double-height ceilings are a game-changer for open-plan family homes. They create an amazing sense of space and let in loads of natural light, making the room feel brighter, bigger and more inviting.

BRING THE DRAMA

High ceilings call for show-stopping lighting – think bold chandeliers or oversized pendants that wouldn't work in a standard-height room. The wow factor? Next level! Tall ceilings also allow for larger windows, maximising views and connecting indoors with outdoors.

HOW TO SOFTEN YOUR KITCHEN

Did you know there's a really obvious way to soften your kitchen and balance out all those hard surfaces and right angles? Just add curves! How many round and curvy items can you spot in this kitchen? Would you believe me if I told you there are more than eight? Yep – the stool seats, the island, the gooseneck tap, the vase, the bowl with artichokes, the pendant, the chopping board and all those cute little vessels on the right side of the bench. And we haven't even started adding up all the cups and mugs in the glass cabinet! You get the drift.

Squiggly candle holders are the perfect neighbour to a squiggly artwork.

Ever wondered what a Coastal Dream kitchen looks like? This!

RENO SCHOOL TOP TIP

If your budget is tight or you're renovating to sell, save on stone by choosing the standard 20 mm thickness. It's budget-friendly, it's still thick enough to resist chips and wear, and it looks fantastic too. If the kitchen is well designed with stunning cabinetry, stylish handles and thoughtful styling, you (or your prospective buyer) will barely notice the thickness of the benchtop!

"I've got too much storage in my kitchen!" – said no one ever.

WONDER WHITE

Can't decide on the perfect white for your kitchen cabinetry? Match it to your wall colour. It creates a seamless, cohesive look that makes your space feel bigger and brighter. Plus, it's a foolproof way to avoid mismatched whites. Fresh, balanced and beautiful!

FUN FACT

Did you know a butler's pantry originally served as a secure room where the butler stored and cleaned the household silverware? It was common for the butler to sleep there, too, to keep everything safe – hence the name. Today, a butler's pantry is a must-have for many home owners, doubling as extra space for food prep, storage and stashing dirty dishes out of sight while entertaining. We don't recommend sleeping in it though!

TO BP OR NOT TO BP?

The great debate: to butler's pantry or not? Lana skipped the traditional BP, opting for a "butler's office" (yes, that's a thing!) instead. Meanwhile, Bonnie and Erin said "Yes way, rosé!" to butler's pantries, adding extra functionality and keeping the family mess out of sight. What's your dream home vibe? Would you BP, or skip it?

SHOWCASE YOUR STARS

Got gorgeous dishes, glassware or heirlooms? Let them shine on open shelving! Just make sure they're display-ready – this spot is for your curated collection, not your everyday clutter. The mismatched Tupperware belongs behind closed doors.

SAVVY SAVER

No built-in bench seat nook? No worries! A freestanding bench seat still delivers the goods without breaking the budget.

LANA'S SACRED SEATING SPECS

Lana says...

"My rear end has tested countless bench seat builds, and I think I've perfected the specs for a built-in beauty. The secret? Nail the height! If you're adding a cushion, always factor in its thickness. My golden rule: the finished height, cushion included, should be 500 mm. Trust me – your bum will thank you!"

SMART STORAGE IN DISGUISE

Don't waste that space under your bench seat. Add hidden drawers or lift-up panels to turn it into sneaky storage for shoes, blankets or board games. Practical and stylish? Yes, please!

WHY KNOT ADD A WALL SCONCE?

Knotted rope sconces might scream coastal cliché, but when they're this cute, who cares? They bring just the right touch of beachy vibes without going overboard (pun intended). Wall sconces are the ultimate wall accessory for any home style, adding a soft glow and a fun way to play with texture and design. So, why knot? Go ahead and add that sconce!

River stones = stylish zones on a budget.

SHED? WHAT SHED?

That's right – when a sleek white rendered wall comes to the rescue, it hides the tool shed and doubles as a stylish backdrop for another alfresco zone! This clever design turns a practical solution into a stylish feature. Use the extra space for a cosy seating nook, a barbecue zone or a sun-drenched daybed. No one will ever guess there's a shed tucked behind that gorgeous wall.

WHACK UP A WALL… OR TWO

Don't rely on your boundary fences for privacy and sound protection – free-standing walls can do these jobs and more! A rendered curved wall defines the outdoor lounge space, and its fun display niche adds extra flair.

POOL PLANS? DON'T FORGET THE PERIMETER!

Planning a pool? Amazing! But remember, the magic doesn't stop at the water's edge. The area around your pool is just as important. Think about space for sun loungers, shaded seating for entertaining, maybe even a built-in barbecue or outdoor shower. And don't skimp on landscaping – lush greenery, sleek decking and feature lighting can transform your pool area into a resort-worthy retreat.

STAY COOL, INSTALL A POOL!

A pool brings coastal vibes to any home, even in the heart of the city – never underestimate the calming effect of a water view. Its gentle shimmer adds tranquillity to an outdoor space, creating an oasis where you can unwind year-round and gather with family and friends. Whether you're splashing around or admiring the view, a pool can elevate your outdoor experience.

GAS STRUT MAGIC

We've been using gas strut windows since we designed our very first house, and holy moly – we've never looked back! They're the ultimate way to blur the line between indoors and out, and the perks are endless.

Why we're obsessed:

- ✓ Unobstructed views when closed (bye-bye, bi-fold frames!)
- ✓ Easy to open – just nudge it and it glides like magic
- ✓ Total space savers – no awkward bi-fold stacks taking up servery or seating space
- ✓ Built-in awning vibes when open, perfect for rain cover
- ✓ And let's not forget: they just look hot.

We luuurve a gas strut window and think you probably need one in your life too. So what are you waiting for? Get strutting!

BUILD IN A BENCH SEAT... OUTSIDE THIS TIME!

Don't say we didn't warn you: bench seats are always a good idea and one is never enough. To maximise our alfresco space, we built a bench seat at one end of the dining table, leaving plenty of room for the walkway in and out of the house. It's the perfect way to seat more people – hello, space for the whole footy team!

STYLING TIP

Matchy-matchy chairs? Not necessary! We mixed different chairs around the table for added visual interest. The trick? Keep them cohesive with similar timber tones so they look and feel great together.

SWEET DREAMS AND FUN VIBES

Who says kids' rooms are just for sleeping? Not us. These spaces should be so much more – think mini escapes where your little ones can dream, play and let their creativity run wild. Start by styling them like any other room: consider the vibe you're going for and how you want the spaces to feel. Inject some personality and sprinkle in the fun factor with quirky, creative touches that make the room uniquely theirs. A well-designed kids' room isn't just a sanctuary; it's an inspiring space they'll actually want to spend time in (and where they'll maybe even go to bed without a fuss – yes, miracles do happen!).

LET LOOSE ON LINEN

Thank the bedding gods, things have come a looong way in the realm of kids' bedding over the past decade. Long gone are the days when every single-sized quilt cover featured fairies or a fire truck (not that there's anything wrong with that ;-)). You can go to town with linen in kids' rooms – create a fiesta of colour and pattern to shake things up and amp up the fun factor.

Wallpaper brings instant charm – no paintbrush needed!

THE FAST FIVE FOR STYLING KIDS' ROOMS

1. **Whimsical wall art or wallpaper**
   Transform plain walls into a canvas of creativity with fun artwork or patterned wallpaper. We used removable wallpaper that can be updated over time.
2. **Creative storage solutions**
   Storage can double as decor. Keep the room tidy with stylish storage options like woven baskets, fun hooks and playful shelving.
3. **Fun bedding**
   We love a pattern clash on kids' beds. Mix and match plush linen with pillows, blankets and rugs for a bed that sparks joy and excitement.
4. **Playful touches**
   A surfboard as artwork? Yes, please! Adding playful touches like this instantly brings personality to your child's room, making it feel fun and unique.
5. **Pops of colour**
   Add a personal touch to the room with customised coloured furniture, walls or ceiling. Painted elements are easy to change over time as your children's tastes evolve.

GINGHAM IS ALWAYS A GOOD IDEA

You can't go wrong with gingham in a kids' room… or checks, or stripes, for that matter. These patterns add a playful, timeless vibe that feels fresh and fun for all ages. If in doubt, use them all! It's an easy way to add personality without going overboard on colour.

Create rooms they'll love now *and* later.

Freestanding solutions maximise bathroom storage beautifully.

OPEN ABOUT STORAGE

Open shelving is the perfect mix of style and practicality. It's a storage hero that doubles as a display space for candles, perfume bottles, plants or even your favourite bath-time book. Freestanding shelves are budget-friendly, super versatile and easily styled to match your vibe – all while keeping your benchtops clutter-free.

PULL UP A PEW

Pop a little stool next to the bath to hold your wine and book while you soak or use it as a handy spot for supervising the kids.

BEWARE THE PENNY-ROUND PITFALL

Dreaming of a sleek mitred edge for your shower niche? Hold up if you've got your heart set on penny-round tiles. While these cuties pack a style punch, they don't play nicely when it comes to achieving that seamless mitred look. Instead, you'll need a metal trim to finish the edges. The good news? You can choose a trim that blends in beautifully – like we did with a white one that's almost invisible. It's all about striking that balance between practicality and aesthetics.

COASTAL DREAM BATHROOM ESSENTIALS

- ✓ A skylight above the shower
- ✓ A view of the bath under a window, for the moment you walk through the door
- ✓ A curved wall for an extra spesh touch

BRING YOUR FAVOURITE HOTEL SUITE HOME

Have you ever loved a hotel suite so much that you wanted to re-create it at home? Us too! Why not design your bedroom to give you all the luxe vacation vibes every day? You can include a bedroom, a walk-in wardrobe, a sitting area, an ensuite bathroom, even a balcony... hotel luxury knows no limits!

VIGNETTE, SET GO!

Create bedside harmony with a beautiful vignette. Group your bedhead with a bedside table that complements its style, mount a wall sconce then add some artwork that ties in with your colour scheme to bring the look together. The key is balance – mix different heights, textures and colours to create a curated look that's cohesive and calming.

Long and luxe
Dreamy drapes for dreamy nights.

ADD A LOUNGE FOR TWO

Nothing whispers "plush hotel" like a sitting area in the middle of the suite. We used a luxe rug to create a distinct zone for lounging and popped his-and-hers chairs smack bang in the middle of the space. They spin to let you choose a view of the TV, the bedroom or the balcony.

THE LION, THE WITCH AND THE COASTAL DREAM WARDROBE

Enter the robe through whimsical curtains and the first thing you'll notice is the built-in bench seat (super handy for pulling on shoes or laying out outfits), complete with storage drawers underneath and a wall light and artwork – because practical spaces can be pretty too.

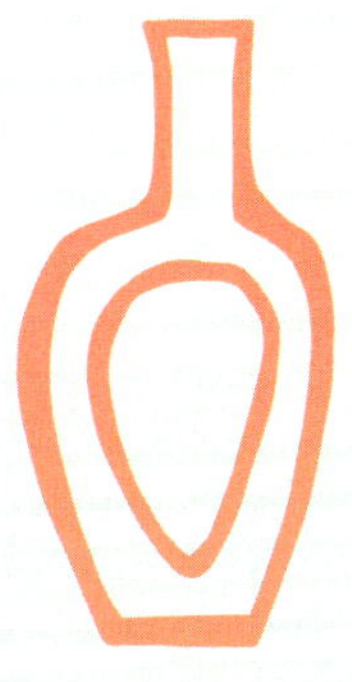

SAVVY SAVER

To save money on wardrobes, forgo the expensive cabinet doors and opt for beautiful curtains instead. They look great and your budget will thank you!

LET YOUR ENSUITE STEAL THE SPOTLIGHT

This dreamy ensuite nails the art of making a space feel bigger and brighter. Here's how you can achieve the same effect.

1. **Go for a walk-around wall:** With access from both sides, it adds flow to the room while creating a soft separation between zones.
2. **Install a wall-to-wall mirror:** Stretching to the ceiling, this clever design amplifies the space and reflects light beautifully.
3. **Maximise natural light:** Notice how the windows, skylight and open layout flood the room with sunlight, making it feel airy and inviting. This is a perfect way to let your bathroom bask in its best light!

REACH FOR THE STARS

A skylight over the bath is one of the easiest design decisions we made in our Coastal Dream ensuite. It floods the room with light during the day and gives a peek at the stars at night. Bonnie and Lana have sung the praises of the skylights over their showers for years, so we knew a bathroom skylight needed to be a feature in our Coastal Dream home too.

REFLECT YOUR RATTAN RUG IN YOUR MIRROR

Want to create a cohesive look in your bathroom? Tie it all together by matching a rattan rug with a timber mirror frame. The natural texture of rattan brings warmth and a relaxed vibe to your space, while the matching elements create a harmonious, pulled-together feel. It's an easy way to add depth and personality, transforming your bathroom into a serene, spa-like retreat.

Go bold with brass
tapware for instant luxe.

HIDE AWAY IN THE GREAT ESCAPE

You know we love a "great room" in a family home, but don't underestimate the importance of creating a great escape too! While the great room is all about open-plan living and togetherness, the great escape is a space to relax and recharge.

Spot the bling! Gold door hinges perfectly match the hardware and add a special touch.

SUPER-SIZE YOUR ARTWORK

When it comes to making a statement, bigger is better. Oversized artwork instantly transforms a room, creating a bold focal point that oozes personality. It's the perfect way to fill empty wall space without the fuss of multiple smaller pieces. Go big and let your art do all the talking!

J'ADORE FRENCH DOORS

An internal wall of French doors and windows will make any room feel extra special. Want three other reasons we think they're the bomb? Sure thing!

1. **Functional:** The double doorway allows easy access. But you can shut them off to minimise noise when you need to.
2. **Budget-friendly:** You can save some serious coin by opting for French doors from your local hardware store. Paint them white and they'll always look like a million bucks.
3. **Classic:** Perhaps what we love most about French doors is that they're timeless. They're always a good design choice and a good investment because they're never going to date.

CALI(FORNIAN) COOL

WELCOME TO OUR "CALI COOL" CALIBUNGI!

CHAPTER FOUR

WELCOME TO OUR "CALI COOL" CALIBUNGI!

Home to a family of five, this suburban Sydney Californian bungalow was in desperate need of some TLC and extra space to accommodate a growing family and their busy lifestyle.

With a dream of polishing their rough diamond into a sparkling jewel, the family handed us their keys, budget and trust. They moved out and we got to work weaving our magic. Our vision? A "Cali Cool" family retreat both stylish and functional for everyday life.

Cali Cool is a relaxed yet refined design inspired by the laid-back California coast. It blends natural textures, soft neutral tones and open, light-filled spaces to create a calm and inviting vibe. Layered textures, ceramics and greenery add warmth and character, while a strong connection between indoors and outdoors keeps things relaxed.

The transformation was dramatic. We kicked things off with a demolition derby at the back of the house, clearing the way for a stunning rear extension and sparkling new swimming pool. The front facade got a glow-up, adding much-needed street appeal. Inside, beautiful bathrooms were added, cosy yet stylish bedrooms took shape, and we created our boldest nursery yet for a beautiful baby girl.

Our favourite part was the emotional reveal – seeing the family walk through their transformed home for the first time was pure magic (tissues required!). This reno was a true labour of love.

AFTER

KEEPING EXISTING ROOF TILES?

Get your builder to check they'll go the distance. These roof tiles started crumbling during the installation of the skylight, so we had to pivot and replace them with new concrete tiles instead of just a fresh spray of Surfmist.

ARCHED ELEGANCE

Why stick to straight lines when you can go for gorgeous arches? These beauties add timeless charm and a soft, welcoming vibe to this entryway. We paired them with patterned tiles for a playful twist that's the perfect blend of sophistication and fun.

SEVEN MUST-HAVES FOR A CALI COOL WELCOME

Your foyer is the first taste of your home, so make it unforgettable with these Cali Cool essentials.

1. **Bench seat bliss:** A comfy spot to kick off your shoes, complete with built-in storage – of course!
2. **Herringbone heaven:** This flooring with its arrow-like pattern draws your eye down the hallway.
3. **Exposed brick magic:** Brings all the rustic charm.
4. **Swoon-worthy storage:** Cupboards with rattan inserts – because practical can totally be pretty!
5. **Dreamy creamy palette:** Opt for a soft, neutral colour scheme that's as delicious as it looks.
6. **Oversized artwork:** Add a statement piece to stop visitors in their tracks.
7. **Nifty desk nook:** It's the perfect little corner for writing, working or just pretending to be busy while admiring your gorgeous foyer.

EXPOSED AND ELEVATED

Let your bricks shine, baby! Exposing existing brickwork adds instant charm, warmth and buckets of character to any interior. It's the perfect way to embrace your home's personality while keeping things effortlessly cool.

OLD BRICKS, NEW TRICKS!

SENSE OF PLACE

Where comfort meets calm and every day ends beautifully.

SHE'S GLOWY

For a bedroom that delivers cosy chic, layer soft textures and a muted palette to create the ultimate cocoon for lazy mornings and early nights. Bring a touch of old-school glam to the ceiling with moulded details, and finish with a statement light fixture. It's these little touches that make this space pure bedroom bliss.

MAKE YOUR CEILINGS FEEL SKY HIGH

Curtains are one of the easiest and most effective ways to soften a space. Here's our secret: hang them as high as you can to create the illusion of taller ceilings. For this space, we installed them just below the cornice, giving the room a sense of height and elegance.

SECRET SPACE SAVERS

Above-counter basins are not just pretty pieces – they're practical too! Because they perch gracefully on top of your vanity, rather than taking up space inside it, you're left with lots more storage space.

AN ENSUITE TOO GOOD TO HIDE

When your ensuite looks this good, why keep it behind closed doors? The pièce de résistance is the custom stone vanity that has pride of place and adds a hefty dose of luxe, while the shower and toilet are cleverly tucked around the corner for privacy.

Peekaboo, there's the loo! And the shower, hidden for privacy.

LAYERS OF LOVE

What child wouldn't love a room that feels like a big ol' bear hug? Mix soft linens, bold stripes and warm neutral tones to nail a cosy yet stylish vibe that will have your little ones actually wanting to go to bed. The trick is layering quilts and blankets and pillows – more is more when it comes to comfort.

HANG IT UP

Say hello to your bedside's new best friend: the hanging pendant. Not only does it free up space for your bedside must-haves, but it's a total lifesaver in smaller rooms or when your bedside table is more about looks than storage.

COASTAL CALM MEETS PLAYFUL PALMS

Smart design choices in kids' rooms will ensure that their bedroom will grow with them. Keep the base pieces classic and coastal (hello, gorgeous striped headboard) then let the artwork bring all the personality. It's giving us serious Cali Cool vibes while still being totally kid-friendly. WIN-WIN!

First freedom: artwork is easily swapped out as kids grow.

SMALL ROOM, BIG SOUL

Can we talk about this stunning Terra Rosa moment? This rich, earthy hue (Italian for "red soil" – how dreamy is that?!) is giving us ALL the warm and cosy feels in this petite nursery space! Drop in a beautiful brass cot to add a touch of luxe that catches the light juuust right. We're obsessed with how this combo creates the perfect little nest for a precious baby girl.

This is exactly what we mean when we say small spaces can pack serious style punch!

Brushed platinum gold tapware is softer than brass and sleeker than chrome. It quietly elevates any bathroom.

SHOWER POWER

Up your kids' shower game in three simple steps.

1. **Double the fun:** Add double shower heads – because showering with a sibling is twice as fun. *Disclaimer... until they're teenagers.
2. **Shelf goals:** Install a shelf that spans the entire width of the shower to hold all their shampoos, body washes and bath potions. Bonus points for elevating the look with a luxe material, like the marble shelf we used here.
3. **Let the light in:** Pop in a skylight. It's an absolute game-changer, flooding the space with natural light and creating those dreamy spa vibes every day.

YOUR POWDER ROOM HERO

Every powder room needs a star, and a statement mirror is always a great focal piece. Add textured wall panelling for depth and character, then dial up the drama with bold fixtures to finish it off. Powder rooms are a great place to have some fun with colours, textures and fittings.

SOFT NEUTRALS,
BOLD STATEMENT.

SHE'S GOT LEGS.

If your kitchen island is the heart of your home, why not make it a statement piece? Adding a feature column, like this classic-meets-modern beauty, gives your bench a touch of timeless elegance and that extra wow factor.

MAKE YOUR RANGE HOOD A MASTERPIECE

Transform your range hood into a standout design feature by customising it to extend all the way to the ceiling... no matter how tall. This creates a dramatic focal point while adding height and grandeur to your kitchen. Make sure to choose your range hood well in advance so your builder and cabinet-maker have the size and specs to design your masterpiece around.

STYLISHLY SEAMLESS

Bonnie says...

"When you're blending different architectural elements – like we did in this Californian bungalow with its Cali Cool vibe – keeping things cohesive is non-negotiable. A tonal colour palette is the secret sauce. It's simple, it's super effective, and it makes the whole home feel seamless and stylish, from front door to back deck."

LAUNDRY LUXE

You'll know by now that we're massive fans of creating laundry rooms that look just as fabulous as every other room in the house. To make this one sing, we've continued the kitchen cabinetry and stone benchtops into the space at exactly the same height so it looks seamless when the door is open. We also added a pop of personality with a pendant light, artwork and greenery.

KEEP IT LIGHT LIGHT, BABY

Don't let your dining pendant block your view of the outdoors. If you're opting for a large, sculptural light, choose a design like this paper-inspired piece. It serves as a stunning centrepiece, adding texture and interest without overpowering the space or obstructing the view.

DESIGN MAGIC

Lana loves...

"Reimagining a floor plan can make the biggest difference to how your home looks and feels – it's a total game-changer! But let's be real, it can also be a pricey fix if you don't nail it the first time. So, take your time, play around with options, and perfect those plans before diving headfirst into your reno or build. A clever floor plan doesn't just look good – it can change your life! This open-plan kitchen, living and dining space is an absolute winner in my books. I went for a similar layout in my own home, and I'd recommend it a thousand times over. Trust me, you'll thank yourself later!"

FAMILY LIVING SPACE, BUT MAKE IT LUXE

Open-plan living is all about flow. Use consistent tones and textures to tie together the kitchen, dining and living areas for effortless style and function. Add a touch of luxury to each zone with statement lighting, plush furnishings and beautiful cabinetry.

TRIM THAT
TURNS HEADS.

RENO SCHOOL INSIGHT

Not all glass is created equal. A key factor in a winning interior design is how your home feels, and the type of glass you choose (or don't choose) plays a big role in that. Ideally, "performance glass" would feature throughout your home. But if your budget doesn't allow for that, prioritise a few key areas where it will make the biggest impact. For instance, if your main living space is exposed to direct sunlight, like in this home, consider glass that reduces UV exposure and harsh glare. Trust us, it's a worthwhile investment – your family (and your furniture!) will thank you. Note that your local council or development approval body may require a minimum standard of glass for energy efficiency, so check with them before you start.

Bonus tip: Decide on your glass early and include it in your builder's scope of work, as your choice will affect your quote.

LOOK UP!

Ceilings aren't just for hiding the roof space – they're your chance to add serious wow factor, from subtle detailing to bold design statements. This one, topping out at 5.4 metres, shows how clever ceiling details can elevate an entire room.

WINDOW TO WOW

Oversized windows and floor-length curtains are a match made in renovation heaven. The picture window frames the stunning water view during the day, while the curtains offer privacy and temperature control at night.

LIVING ROOM LUXE

This plush rust-toned sofa is perfect for lounging, napping, or kicking back with your nearest and dearest. The rich, warm tone adds depth and cosiness to the room while being kid-friendly. Pair it with soft neutrals for balance, and position it strategically to highlight your room's focal points – like a fireplace or a feature ceiling.

HOW TO STYLE AN OPEN-PLAN LOUNGE ROOM 101

1. Start with a large rug to define the space and anchor your furniture – it's like the glue that holds everything together.
2. Use a sectional sofa or some stylish chairs to create a cosy zone, but make sure there's still room for everyone to move around easily.
3. Keep it light and breezy with low-profile furniture, so nothing blocks the flow of conversation.
4. Arrange your furniture around a focal point – in this case, the fab gas fire – to give the space purpose and make it feel cosy and inviting.
5. Finish with some wow-worthy artwork or a statement piece above the fireplace to draw the eye and tie the whole look together.

SAVVY SAVER

Looks like marble, but surprise – it's resin! This gorgeous side table brings all the luxe vibes without the hefty weight or price tag. And the cherry on top? No two pieces are alike so you still get to enjoy the unique charm of marble.

An internal courtyard is a breath of fresh air in more ways than one.

BLUR THE LINES BETWEEN INSIDE AND OUT

An internal courtyard is a fantastic way to create a beautiful outlook from multiple rooms in the house while also inviting natural light and fresh air. Add a lush green weeping maple as a centrepiece to create a calming vibe that's hard to beat.

POOL PLACEMENT

Deciding where to put your pool is a big deal in any renovation, and there are definitely pros and cons to placing it close to the house versus further away. For this home, we chose to make the pool part of the alfresco space, and here's why.

- ✓ The pool feels like an extension of the house, creating a stunning water view right on the doorstep.
- ✓ It's super easy to keep an eye on the little ones while they swim.
- ✓ The grass behind the pool is free for all the fun stuff – kicking a ball, building a cubby house or hosting a garden party.

PERGOLA PERFECTION

A recycled hardwood pergola with a story? Yes, please! This stunning structure, crafted from timber salvaged from the last timber bridge in Inverell Shire (northern New South Wales), adds rustic charm to the Cali Cool vision. Consider using recycled materials to bring authentic character and history to your home.

When the light hits just right and the whole space turns to gold.

PIMP YOUR POOL

Take your pool game to the next level with these two easy upgrades.

1. **Add statement tiles:** A playful checkerboard pattern screams "pool party"! Tile your top step like we have here, or choose a feature waterline tile to carry the fun around the entire edge.
2. **Cushion the edges:** For a chic, resort-style vibe, custom cushions in waterproof fabric (fitted perfectly to the coping) are both functional and fabulous – no more painful scrapes behind the knees.

ROLLING SEAS

THE ULTIMATE BEACHFRONT HOLIDAY PAD

CHAPTER FIVE

THE ULTIMATE BEACHFRONT HOLIDAY PAD

It's not every day you get a call from a world champion! So you can imagine how thrilled (and maybe a little starstruck) we were when three-time world champion surfer Mick Fanning and his gorgeous partner Breeana reached out. They wanted our help to transform their beachfront family home into a holiday haven. And their brief? "Do your thing!" They handed over full creative control – and their trust – to us.

Their home, Rolling Seas, was already an absolute stunner. We're talking three storeys plus a separate guest cottage, perched right on the beachfront at Bilinga on the Gold Coast.

Built by Mick in 2014, Rolling Seas blends classic coastal style with some unexpected twists. The white walls and whitewashed floorboards are exactly what you'd expect from a house on the beach, but the use of reclaimed materials really caught our eye. Timber doors, exposed beams, an intricate wrought iron balustrade and recycled bricks – these touches give the home its own unique character. It's truly one of a kind.

Working with Mick and Bree was a dream – they gave us free rein to work our Three Birds magic, styling Rolling Seas from top to toe, from games room to gym room, cellar to sauna, and loft to lift (though honestly, the lift pretty much styled itself 😉).

We hope you enjoy soaking up every sun-drenched inch of this incredible slice of paradise.

The perfect palette for a surfside pad: Dulux "Feather Soft" with Dulux "Vivid White" trims.

DULUX "VIVID WHITE"

DULUX "FEATHER SOFT"

SECONDS FROM THE SALT SPRAY

Anchored right beside the rolling waves of Bilinga Beach, this spectacular home blends the charm of a European summer with the laid-back vibes of the Gold Coast. It's the perfect spot for soaking up the sun and surf. And trust us – when we say you're close to the beach, we mean really close! This beauty is the ultimate beachfront retreat for those who crave relaxation with a side of coastal luxury.

VIP ACCESS

When you're a world-class surfer, quick access to the waves is key. The white rendered wall between the property and the beach offers much-needed privacy and security. But that charming reclaimed timber gate framed by a bougainvillea arbour? It's the kind of detail that truly sets this home apart.

ADD THE UNEXPECTED

Imagine if the gate here was a stock-standard white one. Yawn! Never miss a chance to sprinkle in something special or totally unexpected – it's an instant charm booster. Little surprises like this turn a good space into a great one.

SUNKEN SHOWSTOPPER

Here's a way to take your lounging to the next level – literally. Sunken seating is a great way to create a cosy, intimate vibe in your living space, indoors or out. It's perfect for a laid-back, conversation-friendly area that feels super inviting.

OCEAN LIFE
CALLING.

YOUR VACAY STARTS NOW

From the moment you step inside Rolling Seas, you're welcomed by serene spaces that set the tone for your getaway. The reclaimed timber doors add a touch of rustic charm, enticing you into the home and setting the scene for the perfectly imperfect, effortlessly relaxed experience that awaits. First impressions count – and they start before you walk through the doors.

SWING & SIP IN STYLE

Now here's a fun way to hang with friends – literally! Install a cluster of hanging chairs facing each other to create a playful zone where guests can swing, chat and sip their drinks in style.

Swing,
sip, repeat.

Laid-back luxury
Where soft curves, warm tones and natural textures do the talking.

SHAKE IT OFF: RUGS READY FOR BEACHY FOOTPRINTS!

Let's talk rugs. Natural fibre rugs, like jute, are a coastal home essential. We used them inside and out at Rolling Seas. Why? They're super easy to shake off and don't show sandy footprints. Easy-peasy beachy chic!

CHECK THIS OUT

In this games room slash rumpus, we echoed the checkerboard pattern of the rug in the cushions and artwork – a playful nod to classic games like checkers. It's all about weaving in little details that bring the whole space together, making it feel fun yet perfectly cohesive.

GAME ON

In the games room, we gave the existing ping-pong table a serious makeover. We had our painter colour-match the table to the artwork for that seamless style. (Could you imagine the eyesore of a typical bright blue table!? #nowayrosé) And yes, a rug under a ping-pong table (and an alabaster pendant above) is a vibe – it elevates the whole look. Don't forget a non-slip underlay!

Notice the pattern play? It's rhythm, balance and repetition in harmony.

PAIRS OF PLAYFUL PRINTS

When you find art that perfectly matches the colours and vibe of your room, you're winning! We were after a playful feel in the games room, and while we often use a big, bold single piece for impact, this time we found the perfect pair of prints to steal the show. Framed pairs add a fun, lively touch, and they don't have to be the same size – just make sure they complement each other in terms of colour tones.

A TOUCH OF SURFING LEGEND

Oh, and that surfboard? Yep, it's none other than Mick Fanning's, hanging casually on a wall. We've styled with surfboards before, but never one owned by a three-time world champion surfer – how's that for a first? Talk about bringing some serious cred to the space!

From Pilates inside to prosecco outside, this space does it all.

RENO SCHOOL TOP TIP

For instant whimsy vibes or to soften a room, sheer curtains are a no-brainer! Hang them high and drop them low – they should just skim the floor for that effortless, floaty look.

GAMES & GAINS

After you've wrapped up the games, it's time to pop into the wellness studio – and trust us, it doesn't get more zen than this. An infrared sauna is tucked in one corner, while the centre of the room offers plenty of space for Pilates, yoga or a bodyweight session.

WHIMSICAL WINDOW COVERINGS

We couldn't resist adding white, whimsical curtains wherever possible in this holiday home – yes, even in the wellness room. We used the same sheer linen curtains throughout the living areas and bedrooms, too, and they're utterly mesmerising as they catch the breeze. Total beachy holiday vibes!

BLOCK THE BREEZE

Want to add a stylish twist to your alfresco space? Beautifully patterned breeze blocks are the way to go. Not only do they bring a touch of retro charm, but they're also perfect for letting in natural light and airflow while still providing some privacy.

GOOD PAIR DAY

Pop a pair of chairs on either side of a mirror, and you've got yourself a cute little moment. Add a small table between them, and voilà – the perfect spot to perch with a book, a coffee or maybe a cheeky glass of wine.

When in doubt, go black and white. It's classic for a reason.

GO BOLD WITH BLACK

Don't shy away from adding black accents to your styling. We've sprinkled them throughout this home and they make a surprising statement in an otherwise neutral space. Black brings contrast, drama and a dash of sophistication, turning your styling from safe to standout in no time. It's also a great trick for softening the impact of a black TV.

CREATE A CORNER CLUSTER

Do you have an awkward corner in your hallway and don't know what to do with it? Here's a winning combo for instant styling success.

- ✓ **Table:** A small console or table instantly gives the space a sense of purpose.
- ✓ **Table lamp:** Add a table lamp for soft, ambient lighting that brings a warm glow.
- ✓ **Artwork:** Hang a striking piece above the table to inject some personality and colour.

Top it off with a vase or bowl and a stack of books. That once-empty corner is now a stylish, functional spot.

B&W TO THE RESCUE

Totally stuck on selecting artwork? We hear you. Black and white photography can be your saviour! The simplicity of monochrome means it will work with most styles. Pair it with a beautifully styled black console table, and you've got a show-stopping corner that's both chic and sophisticated.

LIGHTEN UP WITH LAYERS

This room shows how sticking to an all-white palette can make a space feel fresh, open and airy. Layering different shades of white and soft neutrals (like those blush-toned cushions) adds warmth and prevents the room from feeling too stark. Perfect for creating that dreamy coastal vibe!

SHELFIE GOALS

Who says kitchen shelving is just for practical stuff? Open shelves are your chance to show off! Mix up your favourite ceramics, a few natural timber pieces and some quirky artwork to create a perfectly curated display.

TEXTURE TALK

The star of this space? The stunning combo of painted brick and character-filled rafters! It's a perfect example of how mixing materials can give your space depth and personality.

FEELS LIKE HOME

Erin says...

A holiday home will always feel more personal and inviting than a hotel, plus you get all the comforts of home (and sometimes more!). These drawers house all the gadgets anybody could need, and in both the main and cottage kitchens, we upped the game with high-quality coffee machines, so guests can enjoy barista-style coffee anytime. It's those little luxuries that take the experience to the next level.

Name a better view...
we'll wait.

A PICTURESQUE POOLSCAPE

How do you style a pool with 180-degree water views? Easy: toss in a fun floatie and let the scenery do the talking!

DAYDREAM ON A DAYBED

Beachside holidays are all about kicking back, so styling your spaces with plenty of lounging spots for guests is key. These large sun loungers can be reconfigured into daybeds, ensuring everyone has a place to unwind in comfort and style.

SUN PROTECTION – BUT MAKE IT STYLISH

For beachside furniture, durability is a must. That's why we chose kiln-dried teak loungers – they're designed to handle the seafront elements and still look fabulous. Add an elegant umbrella offering UV30+ protection, and you've got the perfect shady retreat from the Queensland sun.

YOU SPIN ME RIGHT ROUND

A round mirror softens sharp edges, adds depth to the space and reflects light beautifully to make your dining area feel brighter.

MUSTARD MOMENT

In a neutral coastal dining room, mustard washable dining chair covers are the pop of colour you didn't know you needed. They add a splash of warmth and personality while still blending perfectly with the laid-back coastal vibe.

WHERE RUSTIC
TEXTURES MEET
REFINED LOUNGING.

The cutest copper plumbing we ever did see!

MAKE IT MOODY

Can we talk about contrast? This moody, masculine space stands in stark contrast to the light, breezy feel of the rest of the house, with soft lighting that creates a cosy, intimate vibe. At first glance, it might seem like this room doesn't fit with the light and airy vision for the home, but take a closer look – key elements like brick and timber, the repeated pendant lights (borrowed from the main living area just outside) and the light plush rug tie it all together. It's a brilliant example of how to shift the mood while staying true to the overall style of the home.

WORK-FROM-HOLIDAY VIBES

No one likes having to pull out the lappy while on holidays, but it's made a whole lot more palatable if the work desk in your holiday home is a bit funky and totally different from what you're used to at home or in the office.

PARE BACK THE POWDER ROOM

In the holiday home bathroom, less is definitely more. Unlike your everyday bathroom, it has no need for heaps of storage. Instead, focus on sleek, minimal solutions and style it beautifully with fresh towels, flowers and hand wash.

Beachside bedrooms should be made with long, lazy mornings in mind.

GUEST ROOM GOALS

In a holiday home, it's important that the guest bedrooms feel as welcoming as they are stylish: think layers upon layers of cosy textures to make your guests feel right at home. We opted for natural tones and soft linens to nail that laid-back luxe vibe. The rattan bedhead brings in a coastal touch, while the striped cushions and light bedding add to the relaxed holiday feel. Don't forget fresh flowers by the bedside and a rug underfoot for those first morning steps – pure comfort from the ground up.

BALANCE THAT BOLD BED

When you've got a stunner of a four-poster bed like this one, it's all about balance, baby. We paired this rustic beauty with soft, earthy tones to keep things relaxed and welcoming for guests. A mix of textured cushions and throws creates a layered, cosy vibe, while the patterned rug anchors the bed and brings balance.

LOFTY VIBES

In this gorgeous loft bedroom, we took our styling cues from the lines of the original rafters and balustrade. We reflected these architectural features using stripes for the bed linen and the strappy bench seat at the end of the bed.

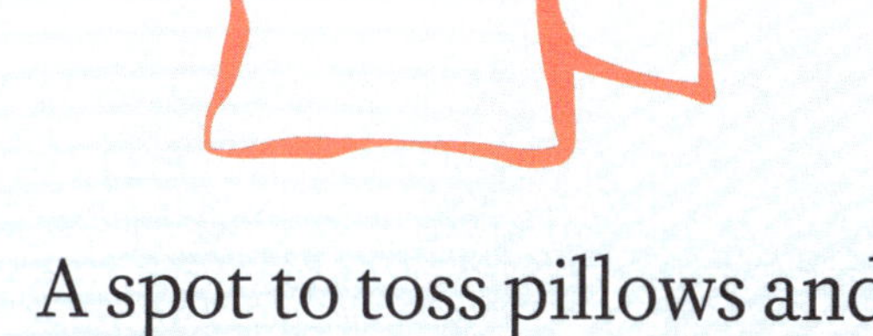

A spot to toss pillows and cushions and tie your laces.

BUILT FOR COMFORT

Our builder crafted three custom beds in the multipurpose room, complete with plush mattresses to ensure a dreamy night's sleep or an arvo nap.

SURFBOARD, BUT MAKE IT ART.

INVEST IN THE BEST

When it comes to guest happiness, comfy beds are non-negotiable. Invest in the best mattresses your budget allows, as this simple luxury is key to a great night's sleep. We went for plush doonas (that's Aussie for duvet or quilt) instead of flimsy hotel blankets to ensure guests stay cosy all night long.

BEDROOM, MEET PLAYROOM

Bonnie says...

"Mick and Bree had the idea to turn the trophy room (yes, he needed an entire room for all that silverware) into a bedroom and lounge combo, and we jumped at it. If you love getting a few families together for a weekend away, you'll know there's nothing better than a room where all the kids can play and sleep. It was a must-have for a fabulous property like this!"

QUICK TIP: WHY WHITE LINEN WORKS

White linen is a smart choice for any holiday rental property – it gives a crisp, clean look that guests associate with luxury, it's easy to clean and maintain (thanks, bleachability!), and it works with any interior style. Plus, guests often perceive white bedding as more hygienic, giving them peace of mind. It's a win-win for both style and practicality.

PLAYROOM BY DAY, BEDROOM BY NIGHT

A checklist for a versatile bedroom and lounge combo:

- ✓ Three built-in beds
- ✓ Sheer curtains for privacy
- ✓ Bedside wall-lights for reading
- ✓ Comfy mattresses for a good night's sleep.

KEEP IT LIGHT, BRIGHT & BREEZY

When creating a relaxing coastal lounge, stick to neutral tones and natural textures for that effortless beachy vibe. Soft cushions, an oversized sofa and a statement timber coffee table ground the space while keeping it comfy and inviting. Want to add a whimsical touch? Hang paper lanterns or a lightweight pendant from the ceiling and sit back and be mesmerised as they sway in the breeze.

See that stairway to heaven? It actually leads to the loft bedroom... but that's pretty heavenly too!

BOLSTER YOUR
BED GAME.

FRONT ROW TIX TO THE SURF SHOW

When you've got a view this spectacular, your bedroom set-up needs to do it justice. Originally, the four-poster bed sat in the centre of the room, but Bon took one for the team and tested every possible layout (yep, she actually slept with the bed in different spots #truestory #hardlife). The winning set-up? Bedhead against the wall! From this position, you can gaze at the surf without even lifting your head off the pillows – hello, lazy luxury!

SAVVY SAVER

Want an easy, budget-friendly way to style your bed? Drape a sheet across it (like a throw) to break up the expanse of the doona cover. Here, we've used an earth-toned stonewash cotton sheet for that relaxed, natural vibe.

While the main house is on the beachfront, the separate cottage holds its own streetside.

SHAKEN, NOT STIRRED

This playful cocktail print is serving up serious coastal vibes!

COLONEL MUSTARD IN THE LIVING ROOM

Remember those mustard linen dining chairs in the main house? In the cottage, we've incorporated linen in the same colour – this time on a sofa. It adds a splash of colour to the room while keeping things consistent between dwellings.

ART THAT MAKES A SPLASH

Bold artwork is the ultimate way to inject colour and personality into a space. Against neutral walls, a feature piece can add an unexpected touch of fun and tie the whole vibe together.

BRICK, BUT BETTER

Painting brick has been our fave reno trick since day one. It's such a quick, easy and cost-effective way to update a space. We love the texture and charm it brings to this coastal cottage interior.

SPIRAL STAIRCASE CHARM

This spiral beauty brings a touch of whimsy that we just love! Its sleek white finish blends perfectly with the neutral palette of the cottage while giving the space a little architectural oomph.

SWEET DREAMS & SUNSET SCHEMES

A sunset-inspired colour palette of warm terracotta tones and soft neutrals is a winner for a relaxed yet inviting guest room.

Meet Sophie Bell,
La Playa, Bali.

THREE BIRDS STICKYBEAK

COME PLAY IN PARADISE!

CHAPTER SIX

STICKYBEAK

/ˈstɪkɪbiːk/
informal

noun: a person who is inquisitive or nosy

verb: to take an enquiring look or conduct an investigation ("They were eager to stickybeak at the neighbours' new reno")

Ready to feast your eyes on some seriously gorgeous homes oozing vacay vibes? We're thrilled to invite you inside a show-stopping selection of properties created by family and friends of Three Birds. These aren't our own projects, but they're stunning homes crafted by people who are close to our hearts and who have generously opened their doors to us.

From dreamy island feels and uber-cool inner-city retreats to a luxurious postmodern masterpiece and even a cosy ski chalet, they're all pure eye candy. Each one is unique, yet they share that magic touch we're obsessed with: the irresistible holiday-at-home vibe.

Enjoy the stickybeak!

Whimsy in the wind
Sheer curtains at La Playa dance with the breeze and gently filter the sunlight.

LET'S GO TO LA PLAYA!

SOPHIE BELL, BALI

Pack your bags and grab your passport – we're off to Bali, baby! Say hello to La Playa, a dreamy duo of villas designed by the one and only Sophie Bell, the founder and creative director of Peppa Hart. Soph's no stranger to a reno or a Three Birds book (remember Hinterland Hideaway from our second book?).

A few years ago, Sophie and her family packed up and relocated to Bali to embrace island life, and she's been a busy bee ever since. Together with her hubby, she's created not one but two stunning villas nestled in lush rice fields. Each is bursting with laid-back island vibes and curated spaces that make you want to book your stay immediately. Welcome to La Playa, where the beauty of Bali meets beautiful design. ***casalaplayabali.com***

PLUNGE INTO PARADISE

The towering palms and organically shaped pool truly bring the laid-back Bali vibes to life.

WILD ABOUT CRAZY PAVING

Sophie was a pioneer of the crazy paving revival so it's no surprise that it features in her latest home.

Island craft Crafted from concrete by Balinese artisans, the open kitchen at La Playa epitomises laid-back island living.

Painted by Sophie herself. Is there anything she can't do?
HAVANA

HANDCRAFTED HEAVEN

This breezy home is filled with bespoke fixtures, furniture and even artwork, designed by Sophie. Her creativity and design magic pop up cverywhere in La Playa.

Soak it up, queen!
This elevated bath is calling your name for some serious relaxation.

APPLES DON'T FALL FAR FROM THE TREE

LINDA AND MAURIE SCOTT, BALMAIN

Bonnie is the design queen behind all our stunning Three Birds projects – she's the one with the killer taste and a knack for dreamy design choices. So it won't be a surprise when we tell you Bon's got renovating in her blood. And who do we have to thank for that? Her incredibly talented parents, of course!

In the heart of Sydney's inner-west, you'll find this gorgeously transformed home by Linda and Maurie Scott, Bonnie's very own mum and dad. These seasoned renovators have a serious talent for turning tired old homes into absolute stunners, and this Balmain oasis is no exception.

They've nailed the perfect blend of industrial New York loft vibes with a sprinkle of Mediterranean charm – somehow, it all just works. This isn't their first reno rodeo and it definitely won't be their last, but according to Bonnie, this one's their "best yet". Come on in and have a stickybeak at this stunning urban sanctuary – it's a beauty!

SET THE MOOD FROM THE STREET

Think of your facade as the cover of a book – it should make people need to know more. We're hooked already!

Meet Three Birds reno royalty: Linda and Maurie Scott.

ANOTHER BRICK IN THE WALL

Recycled bricks add texture, warmth, and a bit of that "perfectly imperfect" vibe we love. A tip from Bonnie's mum, Linda: a quick acid wash will bring out the earthy tones in bricks and create a gorgeous lived-in feel.

BLACK MAGIC

The black island bench adds instant drama and sophistication, giving the whole kitchen depth and dimension.

THE BOLD AND THE BEAUTIFUL

Real marble and dark cabinetry are a match made in industrial kitchen heaven.

THE REAL DEAL

If your budget extends to real marble, Bonnie's mum says, "Do it!" Yes, it requires a bit of love and care, but Linda promises that's a small price to pay for a swoon-worthy surface.

STEEL YOURSELF

The stunning black steel doors were the splurge item in this reno. But if you're looking to save, see how Erin got this look for less with her butler's pantry on page 20.

BRING THE HOLIDAY VIBES HOME

Layered plants, like olive trees, palms and potted foliage, create a breezy Mediterranean feel outdoors. It's the ultimate escape – no passport required!

THE SECRET TO INSTANT FRESHNESS

Make Dulux "Vivid White" your go-to for walls, doors and trim. It's bright without being clinical and gives your space a gorgeous gallery-like finish.

SPOT THE FANCY FLUTED DETAILING.

Be bowled over
A statement bowl or vessel basin like this adds instant wow factor to any bathroom.

Draped towels are the simplest way to bring a bit of warmth and texture to a bathroom. And here's the styling secret – it's all in the artful "I just tossed it there" drape.

BUTLER'S SINKS: NOT JUST FOR BUTLER'S PANTRIES

These beauties are just as stunning in kitchens, laundries and even bathrooms.

SUITE DREAMS

Crisp white bedding and stacks of cushions are the key to that boutique hotel feel. Add floor-to-ceiling shutter doors for sophisticated Parisian vibes.

I'M ON THE BLEACHERS

A dining table doesn't need to be all matchy-matchy to look fabulous. We love how Linda chose a bench seat and styled it with a fur throw for a touch of cosy that softens the look.

AIM HIGH

A soaring void or an interesting ceiling line not only creates a sense of grandeur but can also flood your space with natural light.

FAMILY TIES AND DREAMY VIBES

CASEY SCOTT, BALMAIN

If you thought Bonnie was the only sibling in her family who scored the reno gene, think again! Her brother, Casey Scott, is also a talented renovator. Check out how he worked his magic on this inner-Sydney cottage.

What was once a tiny weatherboard home has been completely transformed, bringing those "vacay-at-home" vibes right into the heart of the city. Casey pulled out all the stops on this reno, nearly doubling the floor space by adding an extra bedroom and two bathrooms upstairs. He also managed to honour the cottage's heritage while adding a modern twist we're absolutely obsessed with. Step inside Casey's slice of city paradise, the ultimate blend of style and comfort.

VACAY VIBES IN THE CITY

Walking into this inner-city cottage is like hitting pause on the hustle and bustle. The soft, breezy palette invites you to relax the moment you open the gate.

Meet Bonnie's brother, Casey Scott.

Can we talk about that playful mondo grass path? It's the perfect way to guide your guests right into your own little outdoor oasis.

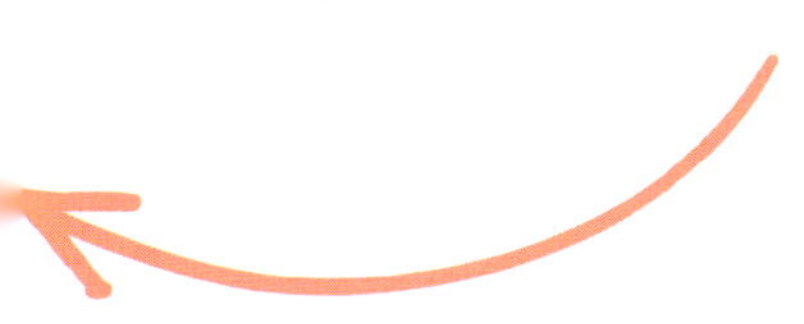

THE ARCHWAY TO YOUR OASIS

If you're looking to add a little magic to your entrance, an arch like this does wonders. Add blush-toned frames for a touch of charm.

CREATE YOUR COURTYARD WITH CONCRETE

We love how Casey balanced the practicality of hard concrete surfaces with the softness of meandering mondo grass and cascades of lush *Rhipsalis*. The perfect mix of structure and nature!

Simplicity done beautifully
Clean lines and natural textures create a calm, contemporary hub.

Colour me happy The soft blush frames add a splash of charm against the crisp white interior and neutral furnishings.

A KITCHEN WITH CHARACTER

This delightful combo of rich timber and stone creates warmth and texture, adding an organic touch to this contemporary home.

STEP UP YOUR STAIR GAME

Stairs can be a beautiful style moment. Add art or a well-chosen light fixture nearby to elevate a simple staircase. And did you spot the cleverly positioned built-in bench seat?

BEDSIDE BLISS

Layered linens and textured cushions make a bedroom feel luxe and liveable. Go for a mix of soft neutrals with pops of colour, and don't forget a cute bedside table to keep essentials and indulgences close.

GO BOLD IN THE BATHROOM

Arched doorways and brass fixtures bring character and a touch of glam to even the smallest spaces.

SAVVY SAVER

Love the luxe look of terrazzo but not the price tag? Go porcelain, like Casey did here! These terrazzo-look tiles mimic the real thing beautifully, are easier to maintain and come at a fraction of the cost.

SQUEAKY CLEAN DREAM

Built-in basin = no crevices, no grime, no worries. Just wipe and go. Germaphobes, this one's for you!

TERRIFIC TERRAZZO

It's back, baby! Terrazzo has made a major comeback, and we're loving the way it adds a fun, modern twist that's equal parts retro and fresh.

AFTER

STICKY BEAK

WELCOME TO THE AMBERS

KAIN BLISS, LAUREN CHARGE AND JENN BLISS, PORT STEPHENS

SQUAD GOALS

Bonnie joined the dream team behind The Ambers for a tour of this holiday haven.

Kain Bliss

Lauren Charge

Jenn Bliss

Meet us at the bar

This alfresco set-up is built for good times – good mates, spicy margs and long, hot summer days.

If you love browsing stunning holiday properties, chances are you've stumbled across – or been lucky enough to stay at – boutique escapes like Salt at Shoal Bay, Talm Beach House or The Beach Abode.

The latest masterpiece from the talented family of renovators behind all those iconic properties is The Ambers, in Port Stephens, New South Wales. This time, the brilliant trio of brother, sister and sister-in-law have transformed their childhood home into a spectacular holiday retreat.

Catering for up to 22 guests, it's the perfect destination for family holidays, weddings, or celebrations of any kind. The Ambers isn't just a place to stay; it's a destination in itself, a dreamy resort-style haven where relaxation and fun blend seamlessly. Every inch has been thoughtfully designed to create an escape like no other, where all ages can unwind, play and make unforgettable memories. Get ready to feast your eyes on some serious holiday inspo – let the daydreaming begin! ***theambers.au***

RINSE.
RELAX.
REPEAT.

YOUR DINNER AWAITS

The blend of soft neutrals and modern Mediterranean charm sets the scene for any casual family dinner or sophisticated long lunch.

OUTDOOR SHOWER GOALS

Whether you're freshening up after a swim or just living your best alfresco life, this set-up is pure poolside perfection.

SLIP, SLIDE, SIP

What could be more vacay than your own waterslide? Add a few swaying palms and you're in holiday heaven. Cocktails optional – but highly recommended.

Cocktails at the bar or dinner under the arch: this home knows how to host.

We adore this
sunken, spacious
and sunkissed
lounge room.

A calming palette, plush textures and the promise of sweet dreams.

PEDESTAL POISE.

HELLO, SUNSHINE

The open-plan kitchen and sunny sunken lounge room are the ultimate blend of chill and chic. Pass the snacks – we're settling in!

SWEET DREAMS GUARANTEED

After a long day at the beach, this bedroom is a big generous hug you can sleep in.

SMALL BUT MIGHTY

- ✓ Clean lines
- ✓ Recessed shelf storage
- ✓ An arched mirror moment

SLIDE INTO SLEEP TIME

The perfect dreamy set-up for the young or the young at heart!

Soak up the serenity
This bathroom is a masterclass in calm and simplicity.

POSTMODERN PERFECTION

ROBYN McDONALD, NORTHBRIDGE

Located in the Sydney suburb of Northbridge, this architectural gem belongs to Lana's friend and neighbour Robyn McDonald.

With a seamless mix of materials – concrete, travertine, limestone, marble, timber and porcelain – Robyn has crafted a space that's both bold and breathtaking. It's no wonder it's regularly hired for high-end photo shoots.

This fabulous postmodern-style home is built around two stunning feature palm trees that set the "holiday at home" vibe the moment you arrive.

We're so honoured to share this incredible home with you. From its striking design to its effortless glamour, this one-of-a-kind house is sure to leave you feeling inspired.

A CONCRETE CANVAS WITH PERSONALITY

Impeccably chosen artwork and furniture, combined with plush rugs and cushions, prove that modern design doesn't have to mean minimal.

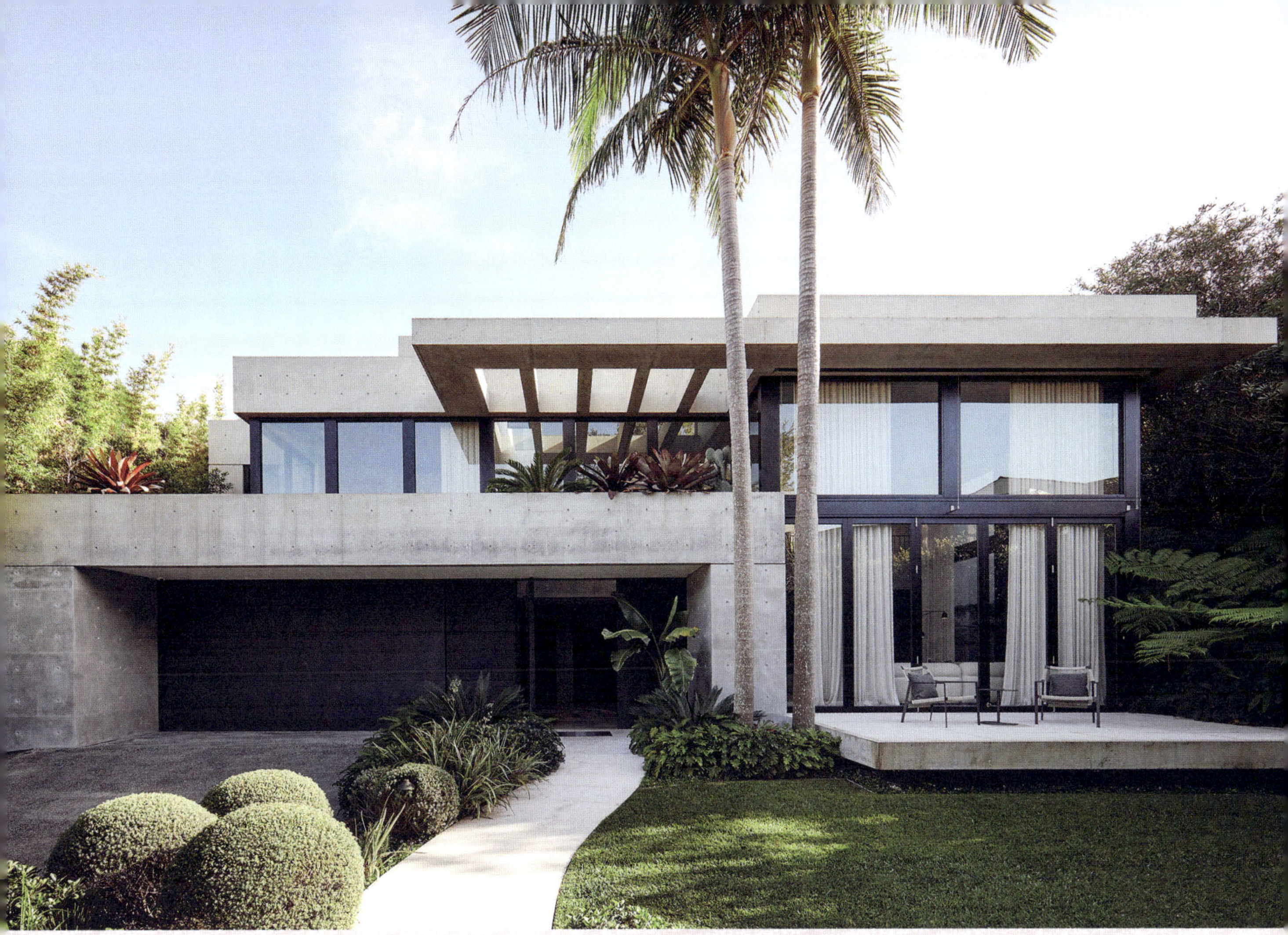

Postmodern magic
Where edgy and elegant live happily ever after.

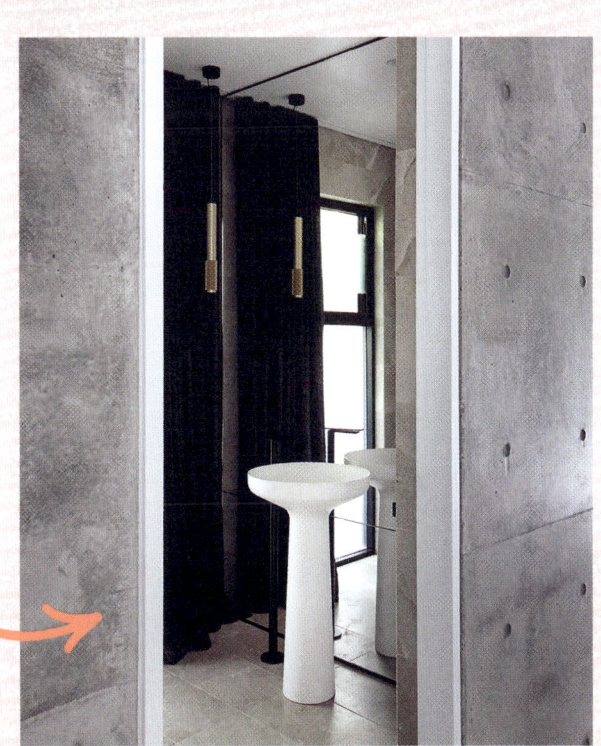

CONCRETE MEETS COUTURE

This sleek bathroom combines hard edges with soft ceramic curves, creating an air of pure sophistication.

The mix of natural light, concrete textures and a forest of greenery viewed through floor-to-ceiling windows makes this space feel cool yet oh-so-inviting.

THE "NON-KITCHEN"

A term coined by Robyn to perfectly describe her kitchen: less conventional-looking cooking space, more cocktail bar vibes.

IF JACK'S MAGIC BEANS GREW CURTAINS INSTEAD OF BEANSTALKS...

Double-height drama, bold art, long dinners.

DINNER PARTY CENTRAL

With its bold leather chairs, modern art and marble flooring perfection, this dining room was made for hosting in serious style.

TROPICAL VIBES MEET INDUSTRIAL COOL

This poolside set-up is the ultimate "vacay at home" dream – concrete chic paired with lush greenery. Who's ready for a dip?

The spot where
architecture meets oasis.

Meet Monique, the lady behind the lens at many of Three Birds' early projects.

A SNOW BUNNY'S DREAM STAY

MONIQUE EASTON, THREDBO

At the Eastern, a breathtaking Thredbo apartment, minimalist design meets the rugged beauty of nature. The Eastern is the creation of photographer and Three Birds friend Monique Easton, whose lifelong love of Thredbo and passion for design shines through in every detail.

Inspired by childhood skiing memories and the calming serenity of mountain vistas, Mon set out to create something truly special: a home that feels like an effortless extension of its stunning surroundings.

Muted tones, natural materials and clean, elegant lines ensure the view takes centre stage in every scene. The Eastern is a tranquil retreat that strikes the perfect balance between style and functionality – a space in which to rest, play and recharge.

Take a peek at this one-of-a-kind mountain sanctuary. ***theeasternthredbovillage.com***

WELCOME TO THREDBO

Blonde timbers, minimalist styling, Scandi vibes... and a perfect place to kick off your snowy boots.

Snowy views and cosy brews
When your view is this good, who needs artwork?

HEY THERE, CUTE KITCHENETTE!

This small but stylish space is perfectly sized for making your morning coffee. Would you believe us if we told you it's made from plywood?

COFFEE + A COSY BED = PERFECTION.

Add a great book, and you're officially winning at life.

LINGER LONGER

Here's proof that simplicity is a luxury. With that enchanting view of the snow-dusted mountains, who wouldn't want to linger in the kitchen a little longer?

APRÈS-SKI

What better way to recharge after a day on the slopes than in this beautiful Scandi-inspired bedroom? Spot the sleek mini spotlights on the timber-lined ceiling.

Beach House H2O
The dream home of Reno Schooler Bec Berrell

SUPERSTAR STUDENTS

BIRDS OF A FEATHER

CHAPTER SEVEN

BIRDS OF A FEATHER RENO TOGETHER

When we created our Reno School and Styling School courses, our mission was simple (and a little bit life-changing): to share all our secrets about creating dream homes – designing, renovating and styling – to give women the confidence to absolutely smash it.

We packed these courses with every tip we've picked up along the way so our birdies can dodge rookie mistakes and budget blow-outs. It's about saving time, money and stress while making the reno journey a joy.

But here's the thing that's completely blown us away: the incredible community that's grown from it! It's a sisterhood of style! Our online community is a total buzz-fest, with students sharing their reno wins, asking for advice, swapping tips and cheering each other on. It's so much more than a learning space – it's a vibe, a tribe and the ultimate support crew. From feedback on floor plans to tackling tricky design dilemmas, these renovation rockstars have got each other's backs.

We *love* seeing our students' projects and hearing their stories – it's seriously the highlight of what we do. Choosing just a handful to feature here was almost impossible! Every single one is fabulous in its own right, but we've gathered a few superstar standouts to share with you.

Get ready to fall in love with these inspiring projects, each one serving serious vacay-at-home vibes – and proving that dream living isn't just for holidays.

Let there be light!
See more of Bec Berrell's stunning home over the page.

BEC BERRELL

NORTHERN BEACHES, SYDNEY

Welcome to Bec Berrell's dreamy beach house, where every detail whispers relaxed vacay-at-home vibes. A proud Three Birds Reno School grad, Bec has turned her vision into reality, blending laid-back coastal charm with family-friendly functionality.

Bec's design is the epitome of beachside living. From the breezy open-plan layout to the lush poolside views, it has everything we adore about seaside sanctuaries. Step inside and soak up the inspo from this stunning home, lovingly dubbed Beach House H2O. Trust us, you'll want to steal every tip from Bec's playbook for your own slice of coastal paradise.

IN BEC'S WORDS...

FRONT ENTRANCE VIBES

I wanted the front of my home to feel like a true beach house from the get-go. The pale grey weatherboard exterior and classic picket fence set the tone, while the lush green plants give it that tropical feel.

If you want to bring that holiday vibe home, invest in comfy outdoor furniture, add a few tropical plants, and don't forget a stylish umbrella for shade.

OUTDOOR OASIS MUST-HAVES

The deck is my favourite spot for lazy afternoons and long lunches. Creating a seamless indoor-outdoor space was key for me, and I love how the deck just flows right out from the living area.

JUST ADD WATER!

When you're this close to the beach, you want a cool, coastal feel – even when you can't see the ocean. My pool is the backyard's shining star, bringing that sparkling water view right to my doorstep. I've paired it with tropical plants like palm trees and frangipanis, plus sun loungers and a big umbrella for those instant coastal resort feels.

Bec's living room screams "beach house" from its white coastal rafters.

BRING THE INDOORS OUT

The heart of my home flows uninterrupted between the kitchen and the outdoor entertaining area. Big sliding doors keep the space open and airy, while a gas strut window makes passing plates out to the deck a breeze. With an outdoor kitchen featuring a built-in barbecue and a drinks fridge, I'm always ready to entertain!

REACH FOR THE SKY WITH A RAKED CEILING

Nothing says "beach house" like a high, white raked ceiling. I added beams and oversized rattan pendants for extra charm, plus ceiling fans to keep things cool when the breeze takes a break. It makes the whole space feel light and airy.

FLOORING THAT WORKS FOR YOU

When you've got sand and surf just down the road, you need floors that can handle a lot of wear. My engineered oak floors are perfect – soft underfoot, easy to clean, and they look like natural timber without the upkeep. They're the low-maintenance luxury every beach house needs.

KATRINA CONNOLLY

PALM COVE, FAR NORTH QUEENSLAND

While holidaying in Far North Queensland, Katrina Connolly fell in love with the resort town of Palm Cove and decided to create a holiday home for her blended family of nine.

Katrina's vision for the new build centred on laid-back elegance. Open spaces, sophisticated contemporary design and minimalist decor are offset by warm accents and furnishings, delivering the ultimate retreat for guests of all ages.

With five bedrooms, five and a half bathrooms and plenty of spaces in which to gather (or escape for some quiet time), this home beautifully captures the essence of tropical luxe living. From the breathtaking double-height living room to the playful outdoor games area, Katrina has created a haven where treasured family memories will be made for years to come.

POOLSIDE PARADISE

The pool is my favourite spot to relax and unwind – it feels like our own little oasis! I wanted it to connect seamlessly with the alfresco areas, so we designed it to run alongside the living spaces for the perfect indoor–outdoor flow.

FIRST DIBS
ON THIS SUN
LOUNGE!

SEATING GALORE

With seven children in our blended family, I wanted our home to have plenty of seating spots so everyone could mingle or find a quiet corner to read. There's a little something for everyone in each seating area, both inside and out.

DOUBLE-HEIGHT DREAMS

The double-height ceilings in our living room give the space such a grand, airy feel. I love how they connect to our outdoor areas and the pool, bringing the tropical view inside.

TROPICAL TOUCHES

A simple colour palette of natural tones lets the lush tropical surroundings take centre stage. To add texture and character, we incorporated breeze blocks and stone cladding into the facade.

BALI FURNITURE FINDS

Flying to Bali to source custom-made furniture was one of the best decisions we made! It brought in unique pieces and saved on the budget too.

Katrina's home is ready for business at the front and a party out the back.

AMANDA DI GIGLIO

MULGOA, NEW SOUTH WALES

Amanda Di Giglio's home is everything she dreamed of for her family – a modern heritage-style haven with a sprinkle of English country charm. Designed with love for her husband, Chris, her two little ones, Spencer and Florence, and their furry friends, this house is bursting with character, thoughtful details and personal touches that make it truly one of a kind.

From the unexpected bold design choices in the powder room to the warm and inviting alfresco area, every space reflects Amanda's love for blending tradition with individuality. It's not just a house, it's a sanctuary – a place that's brought comfort and peace to her family through life's challenges. This beautiful home is proof that when you design with heart and vision, the result is pure magic.

IN AMANDA'S WORDS...

MAKE AN ENTRANCE!

I wanted our front door to make a statement, so I chose a classic black with brass accents. Paired with patterned tiles, it sets the tone for the whole house – inviting and timeless.

DARK COLOURS ADD DEPTH AND DRAMA

I chose deep charcoal cabinetry for our kitchen to create a sophisticated, classic look. The rich tones contrast beautifully with the light countertops and warm brass fixtures – it's a great way to add depth and drama to your kitchen.

Look how beautifully the arch frames the statement pendant.

A HERITAGE-INSPIRED HEART OF THE HOME

Our kitchen is hands down my favourite room. I wanted to create that old English heritage feel with a touch of farmhouse charm. My favourite features? The oversized double sink with a view of the backyard, the pot filler above the cooktop and our classic Falcon oven.

ADD ARCHES, ADD CHARACTER

Adding a heritage arch in the hallway was a last-minute decision, and I'm so glad we did it! That arch inspired similar details throughout the house, from the arbour outside to the arched doorway into our walk-in robe.

HERRINGBONE HEAVEN.

CREATE FLOW WITH OPEN SPACES

Our open-plan kitchen and living area lets me keep an eye on the kids while I cook. Open-plan living is ideal for creating a light, connected feel – use furniture to define zones while maintaining an easy flow.

GO WILD WITH WALLPAPER

This woodland wallpaper adds so much personality to the room! I wanted to create a magical space for the kids, where every corner offers something fun to discover. Paired with classic wainscoting, it keeps things playful but timeless.

JUNGLE BOOGIE

Small spaces like powder rooms are perfect for bold design choices.

MATCHY MATCHY FOR THE WIN

We wanted our garage to feel like an extension of the house, not an afterthought. By sticking to the same style – white weatherboard and a pitched roof – we blended the garage seamlessly with the rest of the property. It's all about creating a cohesive look that feels intentional and balanced.

> If I've learned anything from building, it's to implement the ideas you love. They always end up being the favourite features, even if they take a little longer or cost a bit more – I've never regretted those extra details.

Olá!
Welcome to pure poolside perfection in Portugal.

NICOLA FRAYLING

LAGOS, PORTUGAL

Say hello to Nicola Frayling, a Reno School alum who's turned her family home in Lagos, Portugal, into a dreamy "modern Mediterranean" escape. With her husband and two teenage boys by her side, Nicola gave their property a total glow-up, and the results are 🤌! Think open-plan layouts, a fabulous outdoor kitchen and all the signature Mediterranean vibes we swoon over: terracotta tiles, micro-cement render and arches galore. Over three years, Nicola worked her magic to create a space that's equal parts functional, traditional and elegant, all while nailing that seamless indoor–outdoor living we're absolutely obsessed with. What a transformation!

If you're planning an outdoor kitchen like this, hire a pro who knows their way around micro-cement – good workmanship is the key to achieving a flawless, long-lasting finish.

IN NICOLA'S WORDS...

MAKE A SPLASH IN STYLE

When designing your pool area, keep it sleek and simple to let the water and surroundings shine. We went with soft curves and a pale stone finish to create a calm, resort-like vibe that feels like an escape every day.

OUTDOOR KITCHEN GOALS ACHIEVED!

Our micro-cement outdoor kitchen overlooking the pool is hands down my favourite space. It's perfect for entertaining, and micro-cement isn't just beautiful – it's super durable too.

TERRACOTTA TILES FOR TIMELESS CHARM

Our terracotta roof tiles are a nod to classic Mediterranean design, perfectly blending with the natural landscape around our home. Not only are they hard-wearing, but they also bring a rustic charm I absolutely love. If you're aiming for a Mediterranean vibe, terracotta is a must-have for capturing that timeless coastal look.

GO NATURAL WITH TEXTURES AND LIGHT

To get the warm coastal vibe I wanted, I stuck with neutral tones and natural textures like linen, stone and timber. But the best finishing touch is sunlight! Letting natural light flood in makes every space feel light, airy and effortlessly stylish.

VISION BOARDS ARE YOUR BFF

Sticking to my vision board was the secret to success for this reno. With so many gorgeous options out there, it's easy to get sidetracked. My vision board kept me focused and ensured every piece contributed to the look I was after. Trust me, it's a lifesaver for creating a home that flows beautifully from one room to the next.

CURVES ARE CALLING

One of my biggest design must-haves was a grand, sweeping staircase. Curves and arches bring so much warmth and elegance to a space, and I love how our staircase is a feature from the moment you walk through the door. My tip? Don't be afraid to go bold with curves in staircases, doorways or other architectural details – they add a softness and charm that's simply unmatched.

Yes, opposites do attract! Sleek marble, timber seating and brushed brass tapware come together like a design dream team.

KRYSTAL GIARDINA

MELBOURNE, VICTORIA

When Krystal Giardina set out to refresh the home she and her family had built in 2011, her goal was to fill it with light and personality – and wow, did she deliver!

Krystal embraced the playful and calming vibe of an unexpected colour, from the pink marble tiles on the kitchen island to the custom pink pool tiles – and it wasn't even part of the original plan.

IN KRYSTAL'S WORDS...

PEACEFUL POOL

My backyard turned out exactly how I imagined it. Every time I step out there, I'm blown away by how peaceful it feels. The pink custom-blend tiles I designed for the pool add a unique touch I love. It's my little slice of paradise!

GOLDEN HOUR ALL DAY LONG

A skylight in the main bathroom was my must-have. Natural light is such a game-changer! I would have added skylights to the kitchen too, but the budget wouldn't allow it.

LIGHT, BRIGHT AND FULL OF PERSONALITY

I wanted our home to reflect who we are – inviting, bright, happy and comfortable. Adding more light to the spaces and injecting personality into every detail was my goal, and the result is a home that feels warm, welcoming and perfectly us.

PRETTY IN PINK (AND LOVING IT!)

Funnily enough, pink was never my favourite colour and I had no intention of using so much of it in my home. But its calmness and playfulness are infectious – I soon found I had to add as much of it as I could! In the kitchen I used pink marble tiles on the underside of the island.

PRUE GROVES

BRISBANE, QUEENSLAND

Prue Groves' Brisbane home is a stunning mix of bold design, thoughtful details and sustainable styling. Her renovation showcases the beauty of personal touches, practical decisions and creating a home that perfectly suits her family. When they moved in, it was a modest three-bedroom, two-ugly-bathroom house. Now, it's been transformed into a spacious five-bedroom home with two beautiful bathrooms, designed for both comfort and style. Each room has been crafted with intention, turning their city house into a beautiful family retreat.

IN PRUE'S WORDS...

KEEP IT LOW, KEEP THE CHARM

We decided not to raise or knock down our house, even though it's the norm for Queenslander-style homes in our suburb. It just didn't feel right for us. By working with what we had, we managed to retain so much of the home's original charm and character – and we wouldn't have it any other way!

GREEN DREAMS

We chose Dulux "Canaletto" for the exterior, and I love how it makes our home stand out among all the white houses in the neighbourhood. It felt a little risky at first, but being brave with colour really paid off.

V-groove cladding = extra charm.

FLIP THE FLOOR-PLAN

Our kitchen used to be upstairs, which meant enjoying family meals outside or entertaining was a hassle. During our renovation, we added an extension downstairs, creating a beautiful new kitchen and alfresco area. Now I can't decide where to sit and read my book! These open, connected spaces have brought us so much joy.

IT'S THE LITTLE THINGS THAT MAKE IT LUXE

Don't underestimate the impact of small, practical luxuries. A pot filler might seem like a minor detail, but I love how it adds style and convenience to our kitchen. It's beautiful, practical and something I use every day – one of those little touches that never fails to make me smile!

Never underestimate the joy a four-compartment integrated bin will bring you.

SAVVY SAVER

Styling your home doesn't have to cost a fortune. I discovered so many beautiful second-hand treasures, like crockery and trinkets for decorating, on Facebook Marketplace and in op shops. These pieces add character to our home, and it feels great to give them a second life.

Guess what this drawer hides? A full-size foldable ironing board!

TIMBER TREASURE

Our custom-crafted joinery is unique and brings a special touch to our home. The freestanding timber kitchen island is always a great conversation starter.

CREATE CONNECTION

Relocating our kitchen downstairs to open up to the alfresco area was a game-changer! The indoor–outdoor flow makes family meals and entertaining a breeze. If you're renovating, think about how your kitchen connects to outdoor spaces. It's totally changed how we live in our house – for the better.

PRUE'S MUST-HAVES FOR A FARMHOUSE LAUNDRY

1. A farmhouse sink with a charming skirt
2. A deep benchtop for plenty of folding space
3. A fold-out ironing board neatly tucked into a drawer
4. Pull-out storage drawers for easy organisation
5. Hidden powerpoints inside cupboards for a clean, streamlined look

ZOE GODDARD

TERRIGAL, NEW SOUTH WALES

Meet Zoe Goddard, a Three Birds Reno School grad who turned a peaceful Terrigal block into a dreamy lakehouse that perfectly balances relaxation and luxury.

When Zoe and her husband stumbled upon this 1200-square-metre parcel of land – just a stone's throw from the beach and surrounded by lush nature – they knew it was something special. Their vision? A bright white resort-style holiday house that felt like a retreat for extended family getaways and special gatherings. With multiple dwellings – including a main house, a poolside retreat and a private two-bedroom flat for Airbnb guests – Zoe's Lakehouse has become a space for unforgettable memories and picture-perfect photo shoots.

Say it with lighting
I chose statement lighting throughout to add a bit of drama to each room. It's amazing how much a unique pendant or chandelier can elevate the whole space!

IN ZOE'S WORDS...

MULTI-DWELLING MAGIC

We designed two separate dwellings on the property – one as our family home and the other as a potential rental for when the kids fly the nest. This set-up gives us so much flexibility for the future, with the added bonus of rental income when the time is right. It's a win-win!

PLUNGE INTO LUXURY

The two-bedroom flat has its own private plunge pool, and guests absolutely love it! It offers a little taste of luxury and privacy while still being part of the property.

Adding unique features like this can elevate your guest spaces, creating a standout Airbnb experience that feels exclusive and unforgettable.

INDOOR–OUTDOOR LIVING GOALS

I wanted our kitchen and dining space to flow straight out to the alfresco area, and it's been a game-changer for entertaining. On warm summer days, with the doors fully open, the whole space feels connected and inviting.

SHOWER WITH A VIEW

An outdoor shower by the lake was a must for us! It's the perfect spot to rinse off after a swim or simply enjoy a refreshing moment surrounded by nature. I love how the breeze block wall provides just the right amount of privacy while keeping the view wide open.

KAREN MILES
OATLANDS, TASMANIA

Karen Miles' obsession with all things French runs deep, so it's no surprise her cottage renovation is a beautiful ode to heritage restoration and French provincial charm.

Tucked away in the postcard-perfect village of Oatlands, Tasmania, this beauty isn't just a family holiday home. It's also a dreamy venue for elopements, small-scale weddings, photoshoots and Airbnb holidays.

Karen's commitment to celebrating the past infused every detail of the renovation process, from uncovering convict sandstone walls to sourcing heritage bricks that ooze history. Petit Chateau is the ultimate mix of timeless style and a heartfelt nod to its rich roots. Très magnifique!

Dulux "Fair Bianca" is Karen's favourite French white.

IN KAREN'S WORDS...

CHANNELLING FRENCH PROVINCIAL VIBES

For our colour palette, I drew inspiration from classic French châteaux. Warm whites, soft greys and a wistful Provençal green flow throughout the home. Repeating tones, like gentle greens or warm whites, creates a sense of harmony, making your home feel cohesive and inviting.

MY FAVOURITE FRENCH WHITE

I love simplicity, so I used my all-time favourite white, Dulux "Fair Bianca", throughout the cottage – for the interior walls, ceiling and trims. It's a little-known shade, but I adore its warmth and softness; it reminds me of the gentle white of a gardenia.

GO GREY GRACEFULLY

The day we decided to buy the property, I watched in horror as a handyman painted the adjoining barn a bright faux-Federation blue. Quelle horreur! As soon as the purchase was final, we spent two days pressure-washing it back to its original timber (we've never shied away from a bit of hard work to restore original features). Now, we're letting it grey off naturally in the Tassie sun – it will eventually settle to a rustic look that feels perfectly at home here.

THE BIG REVEAL

One of the best nights we've had in this house was when we uncovered the original sandstone walls hidden beneath layers of plaster. My son accidentally kicked through the render, and there it was – stunning convict sandstone. It felt like the house was revealing its true self to us!

CREATE A FRENCH PROVINCIAL COURTYARD

To create an authentic-looking Parisian courtyard, we took inspiration from the rustic convict stone walls and paired them with gravel pathways, olive trees and wrought iron furniture for that quintessential French feel.

BIANCA MULLIGAN

BROOKWATER, QUEENSLAND

Inspired by dreamy European villas, Bianca Mulligan's vision for her family's new home was all about the ultimate holiday-at-home haven, brimming with Mod-iterranean vibes. And the result? Arches for days, floods of natural light, lush greenery and plenty of space for her young family to grow.

Working alongside a dream team of designers, builders and landscapers, Bianca brought her dream home to life with every detail carefully considered. From the beautifully textured rendered exterior paired with striking black window and door frames to the seamless mix of concrete and engineered timber floors, it's a vision of style and sophistication that comes together effortlessly. Every corner of this home feels like an escape to paradise!

A GRAND ENTRANCE

I wanted the entry to make a statement and set the tone for the whole house. The double doors and wide hallways do just that. If you're going for a Mediterranean feel, go big with your entrance and choose features like arches or oversized doors that give a sense of openness from the get-go.

OUTDOOR MAGIC

We added this statement archway to frame the garden. The hanging chairs add a playful twist – they're a great spot for morning coffees, afternoon reads or just a relaxing swing.

Let's face it: when the Three Birds are your biggest influence, the coastal luxe vibes are going to be strong.

WHITE ON WHITE ON WHITE

I kept things crisp and classic with a white-on-white palette, which lets the architecture and the natural greenery from the bush pop. The look is fresh and timeless – it feels like a breath of fresh air every time you walk in. If you're a fan of clean lines and simplicity, you can't go wrong with all white!

ON REFLECTION: POLISHED CONCRETE

I went with polished concrete floors for a pared-back, durable look that complements the modern Mediterranean style. They're easy to clean, they're super practical for a busy family, and they look gorgeous with our light and airy interiors. For anyone debating flooring options, I can confirm that polished concrete is a winner.

GO MOD-ITERRANEAN

Black aluminium frames and feature steel doors were a no-brainer to add a modern edge to the Mediterranean vibe. They frame the views beautifully and create a stunning contrast against all the white.

LET THE LIGHT SHINE

Loads of natural light was a must for me, so I went all out with massive windows, including a 5-metre void window that we had to crane in. It floods the house with light and makes the space feel so airy and open. If you're building or renovating, don't skimp on windows – they're worth every penny for that bright, relaxed feeling.

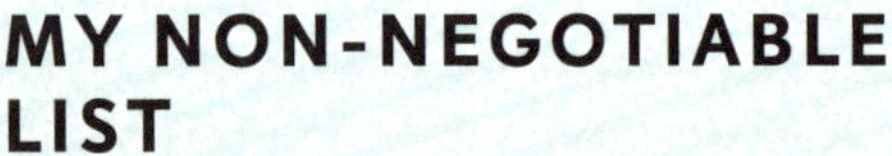

MY NON-NEGOTIABLE LIST

Thanks to Three Birds Reno School, I knew the importance of writing down my "must-haves" and "nice-to-haves" at the very start of this project. Here are the non-negotiables I had to include to bring my vision to life.

- ✓ Arches for days
- ✓ LOTS of natural light
- ✓ Open-plan living with wide hallways
- ✓ Black aluminium windows and feature steel doors
- ✓ Entertainer's pool area
- ✓ Beautiful, low-maintenance gardens with lush greenery and cacti
- ✓ Polished concrete floors and, upstairs, engineered timber flooring
- ✓ Double entry doors
- ✓ White on white on white.

ARCHES ARE ESSENTIAL

To get that true Mediterranean feel, I added arches wherever I could. They soften the space, add character and bring in that European villa vibe.

LISA WEBB

HEPBURN SPRINGS, VICTORIA

Lisa Webb had known of this old gem in Hepburn Springs for years, always dreaming about what it could become with a little love and creativity. When she finally got the chance to make it hers, she rolled up her sleeves and got to work, transforming the "old girl" into St Lucia, a stunning Airbnb that guests absolutely adore.

With its stylish monochromatic exterior, carefully reconfigured rooms and thoughtful touches, this beautiful home has a new life.

IN LISA'S WORDS...

AN OLD GIRL WITH GOOD BONES

I'd driven past this old beauty for years, always thinking she deserved some love to bring her back to her former glory. Her good bones inspired me to start with a timeless black and white exterior, and from there, I carefully planned each room to make the home feel authentic and truly loved.

PAINTING THE OLD GIRL NEW

It's amazing how something as simple as paint can give an old girl like this a brand-new lease on life. The red tones were dated, and I knew a classic black and white palette would completely transform the facade. With a freshened-up exterior and roof, the house now feels charming and timeless.

I knew a classic black and white palette would completely transform the facade.

NONNA NOSTALGIA IN THE KITCHEN

My favourite space is the kitchen – it's got all the charm of a country kitchen and makes me think of my nonna and her love of cooking. She was always in the kitchen, and this space feels like a little slice of her world. It's warm, inviting and full of heart.

SWEET DREAMS

This home was designed with guests in mind, and the bedroom colours were carefully chosen to encourage relaxation and a great night's sleep. The calming green tones and soft textures create a serene space that guests always rave about in their reviews.

CHRISTAL ALEXANDER

NUNDERI, NEW SOUTH WALES

Located in northern New South Wales, Zeb Modern Barn is a striking family home that takes inspiration from New Zealand's Central Otago region. Designed and brought to life by Christal Alexander, this dream home combines bold architectural design with a warm, earthy aesthetic.

With six bedrooms, three-and-a-half bathrooms and plenty of room for a bustling household, the home is a celebration of smart design, personal touches and creative problem-solving. The high-pitched rooflines, lime-washed brick interiors and dark silhouette of the home perfectly complement the lush greenery of the surrounding property. Every detail of Zeb Modern Barn reflects thoughtful design and effortless luxury.

IN CHRISTAL'S WORDS...

HOOKED BY THE LOCATION

We chose this land purely for its location. While most people would've run for the hills, it was the perfect spot for us – close to work, schools and everything we needed. The land itself was completely run-down and overgrown. It took a solid two-year battle to tame and transform it into what it is today.

A ROOM WITH A VIEW

The main bedroom and ensuite are my favourite rooms, hands down. The high ceilings and floor-to-ceiling windows provide an incredible 180-degree view of our property – it's truly exquisite.

A STRIKING SILHOUETTE IN NATURE

I think the dark profile of our house blends beautifully with the lush greenery that surrounds the property. The rooflines, the long lap pool and the eight-person sauna all come into view as you drive down our 180-metre driveway. It's truly a moment to stop and take it all in.

HOW TO NAIL A BARGAIN

We sourced our blackbutt timber from Facebook Marketplace. I kept a close eye out, and when some finally popped up, we jumped on it, driving three hours to collect it. It saved us thousands compared to retail prices!

TRUST YOUR INSTINCTS

The house is entirely my design, and every aspect of the interiors is my own creation. There were countless times when tradespeople advised against certain ideas, but I trusted my instincts and backed myself every time. The outcome speaks for itself. Whether you're building or renovating, it's your home, and you're the one who will live in it, so always follow your heart.

The sheer scale of the windows floods the home with light and a sense of luxury.

INDEX

THANK YOU

As we turn the final pages of our third book, we want to take a moment to say a few big, beautiful thank yous. Because a book like this doesn't come to life on its own – it takes a village, a vision and a whole lotta heart.

To Jane Morrow at Murdoch Books – thank you for your gentle encouragement, wise words and never-ending patience. You've backed us since the beginning, and we're so grateful you nudged us to go again (and again).

To Virginia Birch, Kristy Allen and the amazing Murdoch team – you make the messy, magical process of making a book feel smoother than it should. Your care and support show up on every page.

Amy Anderson, we couldn't have done it without you. Thank you for helping us shape our stories, sort our thoughts and keep the exclamation marks in check (mostly). Your passion for all things renovating and Three Birds shines through in each chapter.

To designer Madeleine Kane, thank you for bringing this book to life visually – your designs make our hearts skip a beat. And to editor Kerryn Burgess, your attention to detail is next level. Thank you for making sure every page hits just right.

To the dream team of photographers – Chris Warnes, Maree Homer, Jacqui Turk, Kristian van der Beek and River Bennett – thank you for capturing our homes in their best light (literally). Your photos make this book sing.

To our Reno School students – we are so proud of you! Watching your reno journeys unfold is the reason we do what we do. Thank you for sharing your stories, trusting the process and proving what's possible.

To our brilliant team behind the scenes – you're the ones who make it all happen, even when we're covered in dust on a building site or running on caffeine. Thank you for keeping the nest humming – we honestly couldn't do it without you.

And to you, our dear readers – thank you for picking up this book, flicking through the pages and dreaming big with us. You're the reason we keep creating. We hope these homes have inspired you to create a life (and a space) you love.

Big love to our fams – the real MVPs behind the scenes. We couldn't do it without you.
With full hearts,

Lana, Erin and Bonnie

Published in 2025 by Murdoch Books, an imprint of Allen & Unwin

Murdoch Books Australia
Cammeraygal Country
83 Alexander Street
Crows Nest NSW 2065
Phone: +61 (0)2 8425 0100
murdochbooks.com.au
info@murdochbooks.com.au

Murdoch Books UK
Ormond House
26–27 Boswell Street
London WC1N 3JZ
Phone: +44 (0) 20 8785 5995
murdochbooks.co.uk
info@murdochbooks.co.uk

For corporate orders and custom publishing, contact our business development team at salesenquiries@murdochbooks.com.au

Publisher: Jane Morrow
Editorial manager: Virginia Birch
Design manager: Kristy Allen
Designer: Madeleine Kane
Editor: Kerryn Burgess
Production manager: Natalie Crouch

Photographs: 172, 173, 175, 176 (l), 176 (r), 177, 178, 179 © Reuben Beeris; 14(l), 16, 22 (tl), 69 (t), 72 (l), 224, 225 (b), 225 (br), 225 (l), 225 (r), 225 (tl), 225 (tr), 226 (b), 226 (bl), 226 (t), 226 (t), 227 (l), 227 ® back cover (lm) © River Bennett; 208 (l), 208 (r), 209, 210, 211 (l), 211 (tr), 211 (br) © Monique Easton; Back Flap, 7, 10–11, 13, 18, 27 (l), 32 (r), 50, 51, 53, 57 (r), 80 (l), 82 (r), 83, 90 (l), 100 (l), 101 (r), 105, 131 (r), 134 (tl), 157 (r), 165 (r), 255 © Maree Homer; Front Cover, 8, 119 © Lauren Schulz; 63, 66 (b), 68 (l), 70 (l), 75 (tl), 92 (l), 96, 97, 98, 99, 100 (r), 106 (r), 108 (t), 109 (l), 110 (b), 111, 112 (b), 114, 115 © Jacqui Turk; 20 (l), 20 (r), 26 (t), 35 (l), 39 (r), 42 (br), 43, 46 (r), 126 (b), 128 (tl), 141 (r), 163, 170, 234 (l), 234 (r), 235 (b), 235 (t), 236 (b), 236 (t), 237 © Kristian van der Beek; 2, 3, 4, 5 (tl, tr), 14–15, 17, 19, 21, 23, 24, 25, 26 (b), 27(r), 28, 29, 30, 31, 32 (l), 33 (l, r), 34, 35 (r), 36 (l, r), 37, 38 (bl, t), 39 (l), 40 (l, r), 41 (l, br, r), 42 (t), 44,45, 46 (l), 47, 48, 49, 54, 55 (l,r), 56 (l,r), 57 (l), 58, 59 (l, r), 60, 61 (r), 62, 64, 65, 66 (t), 67, 68 (r), 69 (b) 70 (r), 71, 72 (r), 73, 74, 75 (rb, tr), 76, 77, 78, 79, 80 (r), 81, 82 (l), 84, 85, 87, 88, 89, 90 (r), 91, 92 (r), 93, 94, 95, 101 (l), 102, 103, 104, 106 (l), 107, 108 (b), 109 (r), 110 (t), 112 (t), 113, 116, 117, 120 (r), 121, 122, 123, 124, 125, 126 (t), 127, 128 (r), 129, 130, 131, 132, 133, 134, 135, 136, 137, 138, 139, 140, 141 (l) 142, 143, 145, 146, 147, 148, 149, 150, 151, 152, 153, 154, 155, 156, 158, 159, 160, 161, 162, 164, 165, 166, 167, 168, 169, 171, 180, 181, 182, 183 (b), 183 (t), 184 (b), 184 (tl), 184 (tr), 185 (l), 185 (r), 186, 187, 188, 189, 190 (b), 190 (t), 191, 192, 193 (l), 193 (r), 194 (t), 195 (l), 195 (r), 196, 197 (l), 197 (r), 198, 199 (l), 199 (r), 200, 201, 202, 203 (b), 203 (t), 204, 205, 206, 207, Front Flap, Back cover(tr) (mr) (br)© Chris Warnes.

Ch 7, Superstar Students photography: 242, 243, 244, 245 © Kristian van der Beek; 220–21, 222, 223 © Belle Escapes Cairns; 224, 225, 226, 227 © River Bennett; 248 (t), 249 (br) © Coastpark Creative; 232–33 © Krystal Giardina; 240, 241© Abbie Mellé; 248 (b) © Tari Peterson; 238, 239 © Grace Picot; 4 (bl), 234, 235, 236, 237 © Louise Roche, Villa Styling; 246, 247 © Leon Schoots; 212–13, 215, 216, 217, 218, 219 © Chris Warnes; 228–29, 230, 231 © Zavial Studio.

Illustrations: 51, 55, 67, 85, 106, 149, 254 Creative Market, Annakaroline; 12, 52, 86, 118, 144, 174, 214 Creative Market, Art Dari Autumn; 92 Shutterstock, Anka Drozd; 1 Creative Market, BirDIY Design; 108 Creative Market, Designwork; 27, 82, 117, 126, 140, 143, 198, 233 Creative Market, Katrinelly; 41, 45, 67, 78, 92, 126, 145 (paint swatches), istock, Nik_Merkulov; 176, 180, 186, 194, 202, 204, 208 rawpixel; 11, 227 Creative Market, Rough Edges Supply Co.; 56 Creative Market, Teresa Art Store.

Murdoch Books would like to thank the following artists, photographers, architects and suppliers whose work appears in this book: 43, 114 Slim Aarons; 206 Kerry Armstrong; 91, 132 BG Studio (Brigitte Grant); 95, 98 Rikki Day; 234, 235, 236, 237 Builder & Interior Design, Front Porch Properties; 24/26 Brigitte Grant for Merci Maison; 20, 106, 126, 133, 157 x 2 Vynka Hallam; 160 Tim Harris; 178 Peppa Hart; 39 Natalie Jane; 202 Nemo Jantzen; 186 James Lane; 190 Scott Ligertwood; 8, 119, 120, 121, 136, 138 Emma Martin; 127 Nicole Nelius for Kip&Co; 106 x 2, 152 x 2, 167, 170 Olive et Oriel; 164 Francesca Owen; 212–13, 215, 216, 217, 218, 219: Rama Architects; 208, 211 Clifford Ross; 11 Louisa Shield; Justine Slough 100,101; 62, 70 Whitney Spicer; 154 x 3 Mario Stefanelli; 151 x 2 Sunday Society.

Murdoch Books acknowledges the Traditional Owners of the Country on which we live and work. We pay our respects to all Aboriginal and Torres Strait Islander Elders, past and present.

EU Authorised Representative: Easy Access System Europe, Mustamäe tee 50, 10621 Tallinn, Estonia, gpsr.requests@easproject.com

ISBN 978 1 76150 096 1

A catalogue record for this book is available from the National Library of Australia

A catalogue record for this book is available from the British Library

Colour reproduction by Splitting Image Colour Studio Pty Ltd, Wantirna, Victoria
Printed in China by 1010 Printing International Limited, China

10 9 8 7 6 5 4 3 2 1